A LIFE FOR
CHRIST

Register This New Book

Benefits of Registering*

- ✓ FREE **replacements** of lost or damaged books
- ✓ FREE **audiobook** – *Pilgrim's Progress,* audiobook edition
- ✓ FREE information about new titles and other **freebies**

www.anekopress.com/new-book-registration

*See our website for requirements and limitations.

A LIFE FOR
CHRIST

What the Normal Christian
Life Should Look Like

D. L. Moody.

ANEKO
PRESS

We love hearing from our readers. Please contact us
at www.anekopress.com/questions-comments with
any questions, comments, or suggestions.

A Life for Christ – Dwight L. Moody

Revised Edition Copyright © 2017

First edition published as *To the Work!, To the Work!* in 1884

Cover Design: Natalia Hawthorne, BookCoverLabs.com

Cover Photography: Jasmin Awad/Shutterstock

Editors: Donna Sundblad and Ruth Zetek

Aneko Press

www.anekopress.com

Aneko Press, Life Sentence Publishing, and our logos are trademarks of
Life Sentence Publishing, Inc.
203 E. Birch Street
P.O. Box 652
Abbotsford, WI 54405

RELIGION / Christian Life / Spiritual Growth

Paperback ISBN: 978-1-62245-475-4

eBook ISBN: 978-1-62245-476-1

10 9 8 7 6 5 4 3 2

Available where books are sold

Contents

*This updated edition of To the Work! To the Work!
is dedicated to the Christian who desires to life a life
for Christ, for His glory and honor.*

Chapter 1

Take Away the Stone

In the gospel of John, we read that at the tomb of Lazarus, our Lord said to His disciples, *Take ye away the stone* (John 11:39). Before the act of raising Lazarus could be performed, the disciples had their part to do. Christ could have removed the stone with a word and easily commanded it to roll away. It would have obeyed His voice, like the dead Lazarus did when He called him back to life. But the Lord wants His children to learn this lesson: They have something to do towards raising the spiritually dead. The disciples not only had to take away the stone, but after Christ raised Lazarus they were told to also *loose him, and let him go* (John 11:44).

Consider this question: how often are people converted without God using some human instrument in some way? God could easily convert all men without us, but that isn't His way.

The stone I want to talk about is a stone that must be rolled away before any great work of God can be accomplished. It is the wretched stone of prejudice. Many people have a huge prejudice against revivals. They hate the very word. And I am sorry to say this feeling isn't confined to the ungodly or people who couldn't care less. The truth is, there happens to be quite a few Christians who seem to hold a strong dislike both toward the word *revival* and to the event itself.

What does revival mean? It simply means a recalling from obscurity – a finding of some hidden treasure and bringing it back to the light. We all must acknowledge that we are living in a time of need. I doubt if there is a family in the world that doesn't have a relative who needs salvation whom they'd like to see brought into the fold of God.

People are eager for a revival in business because of the current widespread and general stagnation in business. People are also concerned that there be a revival of trade, while in politics, we see a great revival right now. In all areas of life, you find people eager for a revival in the things that concern them most.

If this is logical, then I have to ask if it isn't perfectly valid to say that every child of God should be praying for and desiring a revival of godliness in the world at the present time. Don't we need a revival of downright honesty, truthfulness, uprightness, and self-control? In these times, many have become alienated from God and from the house of the Lord and are forming an attachment to visiting the neighborhood bar. Aren't our children being drawn away by hundreds and thousands, so that while the churches are empty, the liquor shops are crowded every Saturday afternoon and evening? I'm sure barkeepers are glad to have a revival in their business. They don't object to selling more whisky and beer. In the same line of thinking then, surely every true Christian should desire that people who are in danger of perishing eternally should be saved and rescued.

Some people seem to think revivals are a modern invention that have come about in recent years, but they are nothing new. If there isn't scriptural authority for revivals, then I don't understand my Bible.

But for the first two thousand years of the world's history, people had no revival that we know of. Probably, if they had, the world wouldn't have been destroyed by the flood. The first real awakening which we read about in the Old Testament was when Moses was sent to Egypt to bring his Hebrew brethren out of the house of bondage. When Moses arrived in Goshen, there must have been a great commotion as many out-of-the-ordinary things were being done. Among the many miracles worked at the hand of God, three million Hebrews were put behind the blood of the slain lamb. This was nothing but God reviving His work among them.

Many today shake their wise heads as if the work of God is nothing but a fad and say the work will not last.

Under Joshua, the Hebrews experienced a great revival and then again under the judges. God constantly revived the Jewish nation in those olden times. Samuel brought the people to Mizpah, and told them to put away their strange gods. Then the Israelites went out and defeated the Philistines, so that they never came back in his day. Dr. Bonar says it may be that David and Jonathan were converted under that revival in the time of Samuel.

Consider the days of Elijah. What else can that be called but a great revival? The people had turned away from God to idolatry, and the prophet summoned them to Mount Carmel. As the multitude stood on the mountain, God answered with fire. *And seeing it, all the people fell on their faces, and they said, The LORD, he is the God; the LORD, he is the God* (1 Kings 18:39). That was the nation turning back to God. Even with this great revival, no doubt some people talked against the work and said it wouldn't last. That is the cry of many today and has been the cry for four thousand years. In the days of Elijah, some old Carmelite probably said, "This won't be permanent." In the same way, many today shake their wise heads as if the work of God is nothing but a fad and say the work will not last.

When we come to New Testament times, we have the

example of the wonderful revival under John the Baptist. Was there ever a man who accomplished so much in a few months, except for the Master Himself? The preaching of John was like the breath of spring after a long and dreary winter. For four hundred long years, the nation of Israel had no prophet and darkness had settled on the nation. John's arrival was like the flashing of a brilliant meteor which heralded the coming day. He didn't preach in the temple or in any synagogue, but on the banks of the Jordan. Men, women, and children flocked to hear him. Almost anyone can draw an audience in a crowded city, but this was out in the desert away from the populated areas. No doubt, this generated great excitement. I suppose the towns and villages were nearly empty as the people flocked to hear the preaching of John.

People are so afraid of excitement. When I went over to England in 1867, I was asked to go and preach at the Derby Racecourse. I saw more excitement there in one day than in all the religious meetings I ever attended in my life put together. And yet I heard no one complaining about too much excitement.

Not long ago, I heard about a minister who attended a public dance until after five o'clock in the morning. The next Sunday he preached against the excitement of revivals – against the late hours, and so on. It wasn't a consistent kind of reasoning.

Also, when you look at the first Pentecost following Christ's resurrection, the apostles preached and you know the result. I suppose the worldly men of that day said it would all die away. Although they brought about the martyrdom of Stephen and James, other men rose up to take possession of the field. From the very place where Stephen was slain, Saul took up the work, and it has been going on ever since.

Many professing Christians find fault and criticize all the time. They criticize the preaching or the singing. Prayers are either too long or too short, too loud or not loud enough. They find fault with the reading of the Word of God or complain that it wasn't the right portion of Scripture. They criticize the preacher, saying things like, "I don't like his style." If you doubt what I'm saying, listen to the people as they go out from a revival meeting or any other religious gathering.

"What did you think of the preacher?" one asks.

"Well, I must confess I was disappointed. I didn't like his approach. He wasn't graceful in his actions."

Another will find a different fault. "He's not logical. I like logic."

Or another may complain, "He didn't preach enough about repentance."

If a preacher doesn't cover every doctrine in every sermon, people begin to find fault. They say, "There was too much repentance and no gospel," or, "It was all gospel and no repentance." "He spoke a great deal about justification, but he said nothing about sanctification." So, if a preacher doesn't go right through the Bible from Genesis to Revelation in one sermon, they instantly find fault and proceed to criticize.

> If a preacher doesn't cover every doctrine in every sermon, people begin to find fault.

Someone with this mindset might say, "The man didn't touch my heart at all." Another may say, "He was all heart and no head. I like a man to preach to my intellect." Or, "He appeals too much to the will. He doesn't give enough importance to the doctrine of election." Or, again, "There is no backbone in his preaching. He doesn't stress doctrine sufficiently." Or, "He's not eloquent." Such complaints go on and on.

You can find hundreds of such faultfinders among professed Christians, but all their criticism won't lead a single soul to Christ. I've never preached a sermon yet that I couldn't pick to pieces and find fault with. I feel Jesus Christ should have a far better representative than me. But I've lived long enough to discover there's nothing perfect in this world. If you plan to wait until you find a perfect preacher or perfect meetings, I'm afraid you'll have to wait until the millennium arrives. What we want is to be looking up to Jesus, so let's be done with faultfinding. When I hear people complain in the way I've described, I say to them, "Come and do better yourself. Step up here and see what you can do." It is so easy to find fault. It takes neither brains nor heart.

Some years ago, a pastor of a little church in a small town became exceedingly discouraged, and brooded over his troubles to such an extent that he became a chronic grumbler. He found fault with his fellow believers because, to his thinking, they didn't treat him well. A fellow minister was invited to assist him a few days in a special service. At the close of the Sunday morning service, our unhappy brother invited the minister to his house for dinner. While they were waiting alone in the living room, he began to share his story. "My brother, you have no idea of my troubles. One of the greatest is that my fellow believers in the church treat me very badly." The other offered the following questions:

"Did they ever spit in your face?"

"No, they haven't come to that."

"Did they ever strike you?"

"No."

"Did they ever crown you with thorns?"

This last question he couldn't answer. Instead, he bowed his head thoughtfully. The fellow minister replied, "Your Master and mine was treated in this way, and all His disciples fled and left Him in the hands of the wicked. Yet He didn't open His mouth to complain."

The effect of this conversation was wonderful. Both ministers bowed in prayer and sincerely sought to follow the mind of Christ Jesus. During the meetings of the ten-day revival, the discontented pastor became wonderfully changed. He worked and prayed with his friend, and many souls were brought to Christ.

Some weeks later, a deacon of the church wrote to the visiting minister and said, "Your recent visit and conversation with our pastor has brought about a wonderful influence for good. We never hear him complain now, and he works more prayerfully and zealously."

Another charge brought against revivals is that they are out of the regular routine. Well, there is no doubt about that. But that doesn't make them wrong. Eldad and Medad were out of the regular succession. *But there remained two of the men in the camp, the name of the one was Eldad and the name of the other Medad, upon whom the spirit also rested; and they were of those that were written, but they had not gone unto the tabernacle; and they began to prophesy in the camp* (Numbers 11:26). Joshua wanted Moses to rebuke them. Instead, Moses said, *It would be good that all the LORD's people were prophets and that the LORD would put his spirit upon them!* (Numbers 11:29).

Elijah and Elisha didn't belong to the regular school of prophets, yet they exercised a mighty influence in their day. John the Baptist didn't follow the regular route. He got his theological training out in the desert. Jesus Christ Himself was out of the recognized order. When Philip told Nathaniel that he had found the Messiah, he said to him, *Can any good thing come out of Nazareth?* (John 1:46).

As we read the history of the past few centuries, we find God has frequently used those who were, so to speak, out of the regular line, order, or method. Martin Luther had to break through the regular order of things in his day before he brought about the mighty Reformation. Now we have some sixty million people who belong to the Lutheran church. John Wesley and George Whitefield weren't exactly operating in the regular method, but look at the mighty work they accomplished.

When God works, things will often be done outside the regular methods. It seems to me that's a good thing, because apparently, some people can't be reached through the regular channels – but they will come to revival meetings which are out of the usual routine. It's true, we've got our churches, but we want to make an effort to reach the outlying masses who won't step foot in a church. Many of these people will come to these meetings simply because they are only held for a few days. And so, if they are to come at all, they must come to a decision about it quickly.

Others come out of idle curiosity or a desire to know what is going on. And often, at the first meeting, something that is said or sung touches them spiritually. If they have come and they hear the gospel, they will probably become real Christians. Sometimes you'll hear people say, "We have our churches. If people won't come to them, let them keep out." But that was not the spirit of the Master when He walked on earth.

When our Civil War broke out we had a very small standing army and so the government asked for volunteers to enlist. Several hundred thousand men came forward and joined the ranks of the regular army, and each man had plenty to do. These volunteers weren't as well trained and drilled as the more experienced soldiers, but both the irregular and regular soldiers were useful. In fact, many of these less-trained volunteers soon became efficient soldiers and performed a great service for the cause of the nation. If the outlying masses of the people are to be reached, we must have both the regulars and the irregulars.

I remember hearing about a Sunday school where the teacher had fallen into a rut. A young man was placed in charge as superintendent, and he wanted to rearrange the seats. Some of the older members said the seats had been in their present position for so many years that they shouldn't be moved. There's a good deal of that kind of spirit today, and it seems to me that if one method isn't successful in reaching people for Christ, we ought to give it up and try some other plan that may be more likely to succeed. If the people won't come to the "regular channels of grace," let's adopt some means that will reach and win them.

Let's not fall into the trap of finding fault because things aren't done exactly like they've been done in the past, or like we think they ought to be done. I am sick and tired of those who constantly complain. Let's pay no attention to them and move forward with the work God has given us to do.

Another very serious charge brought against revivals is that "the work will not last." As I have said, I'm sure there were many on the day of Pentecost who said that. And when Stephen was stoned to death, James beheaded, and finally all the apostles put to death, no doubt those same doubters would call Pentecost a stupendous failure. But was it a failure? Aren't the fruits of that revival at Pentecost still evident even in our time? *Then Peter said unto them, Repent and be baptized each one of you into the name of Jesus Christ for the remission of sins, and ye shall receive the gift of the Holy Spirit. For the promise is unto you and to your children and to all that are afar off, even as many as the Lord our God shall call* (Acts 2:38-39).

Aren't the fruits of that revival at Pentecost still evident even in our time?

In the eyes of the world, the mission of John the Baptist may have also been thought a failure when he was beheaded at the command of Herod, but it wasn't a failure in the sight of heaven. The influence of this wilderness prophet is still felt in the church today. The world also thought Christ's life was a failure as He hung on the cross and died, but in the sight of God it was altogether different. God made the wrath of men to praise Him.

I've got little sympathy for those pastors who begin to preach against revivals when God is reviving the churches. There isn't a single denomination in Christendom today that hasn't sprung out of a revival. The Roman Catholics and the Episcopalians both claim to be apostolic in their origin; if they are, they sprang out of the revival at Pentecost. The Methodist body rose out of revivals under John Wesley and George Whitefield, and didn't the Lutheran church come from the great awakening that swept through Germany in the days of Luther? Wasn't Scotland stirred through the preaching of John Knox? And where did the Quakers come from, if not from the work of God under George Fox? Yet people are so concerned that the regular routine of things might be disturbed. Let's pray that God raises up many to be used by Him for the reviving of His church in our day. I think we need it.

One time we went into a place where one of the ministers found his church opposed to his taking part in the revival meetings. He was told that if he identified himself with the movement, he would alienate some of his congregation. He took the church record and found four-fifths of the members of the church had been converted in times of revival, among them the superintendent of the Sunday school, all the officers of the church, and nearly every active member. The minister went into the church the following Sunday and preached a sermon on revivals, reminding them of what had taken place in the history of the congregation. You will find many who talk against revivals have themselves been converted during such a time.

Not long ago, a capable minister preached a sermon against these awakenings. He didn't believe in revivals. Some of his people searched the church records for the previous twelve years to see how many were added to the membership on profession of their faith. Not a single soul had joined the church in all those years on profession of faith. No wonder the minister of a church like that preached against revivals.

In my experience, those who are converted in a time of special spiritual interest become even stronger Christians than those brought into the church during ordinary times. One young convert helps another, and they get a better start in the Christian life when there are a good many growing together.

People say the converts won't live on in the faith. Well, even under the preaching of Jesus Christ not everyone persisted. *Many of his disciples went back and walked no more with him* (John 6:66). Paul mourned over the fact that some of those who made a profession were walking like enemies of the cross of Christ.

In His wonderful parable found in Matthew 13, the Master shows various kinds of hearers: the stony-ground hearers, the thorny-ground hearers, and the good-ground hearers. Such people will exist until the end of time. I have a fruit tree at my home, and every year it has so many blossoms that if they all produced apples the tree would break. But I'd guess about nine-tenths of the blossoms fall off, and I still have a large number of apples.

Many who make a profession of Christianity fall away. Sometimes those who show the most favorable promise turn out the worst, and those who don't show much potential at the start turn out best in the end. God must prepare the ground, and He must give the increase. *Those along the way are those that hear; then comes the devil and takes away the word out of their hearts, lest they should believe and be saved. Those on the rock are those that when they hear, receive the word with joy, but these have no root, who for a while believe and in time of temptation fall away. And that which fell among thorns are those who when they have heard go forth and are choked with cares and riches and pleasures of this life and bring no fruit to perfection. But that on the good ground are those who in an honest and good heart, having heard the word, keep it and bring forth fruit with patience* (Luke 8:12-15).

I have often said that if I had to convict men of sin, I would have given up the job long ago. That is the work of the Holy Spirit. Our part is to scatter the good seed of the Word, and expect that God will bless it to the saving of men's souls.

Of course, we can't expect much help from those who speak against revivals all the time. I believe the faith of many young disciples becomes chilled by those who condemn these special efforts. If the professed converts don't continue in Christ, it isn't always their own fault.

I preached in a certain city some time ago, and a minister said to me, "I hope this work doesn't turn out like the revival here five years ago. I accepted one hundred converts into the church, and, with the exception of one or two, I don't know where they are today." How discouraging.

I mentioned this to another minister in the same city and said I'd rather give up the work and go back to a secular job, if the fruit of the work wasn't going to last. He said, "I took in one hundred converts at the same time, and I can lay my hand on ninety-eight out of the hundred. For five years, I've watched them and only two have fallen away." Then he asked me if his brother minister had told me what took place in his church after they brought in those young converts. Some of them thought they ought to have a better church, and they became divided among themselves. Nearly all the members left the church. If anyone will just engage wholeheartedly in this work, they will have enough to encourage them.

It's very easy for people to talk against a work like this, but we generally find that these people not only do nothing for the Lord themselves, but they also know nothing about the very thing they are criticizing. Surely, it's hardly fair to condemn a work if we haven't taken the trouble to become personally acquainted with it. Instead of sitting on the platform and simply looking on or criticizing, if such people would mingle among the people and talk to them about their souls, they would quickly see for themselves whether the work was real or not.

I heard about a man who returned from living in India. While out at dinner with some friends one day, he was asked about missions. He said he'd never seen a native convert in all the time he was in India. A missionary sitting at the table with him didn't reply directly to the statement but quietly asked the skeptical Englishman if he had seen any tigers in India. The man rubbed his hands, as if the recollection gave him a good deal of pleasure. He said, "Tigers! Yes, I did. I've shot a good many of them."

The missionary said, "Well, I was in India for a number of years and never saw a tiger." The fact was that the one had been looking for converts and the other for tigers, and they both found what they looked for.

If we look for converts, we will find them. There's no doubt about that. But the truth is that in most cases those who talk against revivals know nothing about them from personal contact or experience. Do you think new converts are going to come around to your house and knock at the door to tell you they've been converted? If you wish to find out the truth about what is happening, you must go among them in their homes and talk to them.

I hope no one reading this book will be afraid of the inquiry room. It is just a tool, a place to answer questions and help lead a soul to Christ once they come forward. At one of the places where I worked, I found many people hated the very name "inquiry room," but no matter what you call it, I argue that it is a perfectly acceptable thing. When a boy is at school and can't solve some problem in algebra, he asks help of someone who knows it. In our case, we are talking about the great question of eternal life which must be solved by each of us. Why shouldn't we ask those who are more experienced than ourselves to help us if they can? If we have any difficulty we can't overcome, in going to others, we will probably find some godly man or woman who experienced that same difficulty twenty years before, and they will be glad to help us. They'll be able to tell us how they were enabled to overcome it. So, don't be afraid to let them help you.

I believe that for every spiritual difficulty there is some promise in the Word of God to meet that difficulty. But if you keep your feelings and your troubles all locked up, how are you to be helped? I might stand and preach to you for thirty days without touching on your particular difficulty. But a twenty-minute private conversation can clear away all your doubts and troubles.

I recently saw a lady who worked in the inquiry room when we were in the south of London nine years ago. She told me she had a list of thirty-five cases of people with whom she talked that she thought were truly converted. She wrote letters to them and sent them little gifts at Christmas and so far as she could tell, not a single one of the thirty-five had wandered away from the faith. She placed her life alongside theirs all these years, and she has been able to be a blessing to them.

If we had a thousand people like this, by the help of God, we'd see signs and wonders. There's no category of people, however hopeless or disgraced, who can't be reached. We must only step out of our comfort zone to reach them. Many Christians are asleep, and we want to arouse them so they will take a personal interest in those living in carelessness and sin. Let's lay aside all our prejudices. If God is working, it hardly matters whether or not the work is done in the exact way we would like to see it done, or in the way we've seen it done in the past.

Let us give up one united cry to God, asking that He revive His work in our midst. Let the work of revival begin with us who are Christians. Let us remove all the hindrances that come from ourselves. Then, by the help of the Spirit, we will be able to reach these non-churchgoers, and multitudes will be brought into the kingdom of God.

Chapter 2

Love, the Motive and Power for Service

Let me call your attention to the thirteenth chapter of Paul's first letter to the Corinthians. As we read this passage, let's use the word *love* instead of the original word *charity*. *Though I speak with the tongues of men and of angels and have not love, I am become as sounding brass or a tinkling cymbal. And though I have the gift of prophecy and understand all mysteries and all knowledge, and though I have all faith, so that I could remove mountains, and have not love, I am nothing. And though I bestow all my goods to feed the poor and though I give my body to be burned and have not love, it profits me nothing* (vv. 1-3).

It's great to be a prophet like Daniel, Isaiah, Elijah, or Elisha, but it is greater, we are told here, to be full of love than to be filled with the spirit of prophecy. Mary of Bethany, who was so full of love, held a higher position than these great prophets did.

*Love suffers long and is benign; love envies not;
love does nothing without due reason, is not puffed
up, is not injurious, seeks not her own, is not easily provoked, thinks no evil, rejoices not in iniquity,*

*but rejoices in the truth; bears all things, believes
all things, hopes all things, endures all things. Love
is never lost, but prophecies shall come to an end,
tongues shall cease, and knowledge shall come to an
end. For we know in part, and we prophesy in part.
But when that which is perfect is come, then that
which is in part shall be done away. When I was a
child, I spoke as a child, I understood as a child, I
thought as a child; but when I became a man, I put
away childish things. For now we see as through a
mirror, in darkness, but then we shall see face to face;
now I know in part, but then I shall know even as
I also am known. And now abide faith, hope, love,
these three; but the greatest of these is love.* (vv. 4-13)

The Enemy had found his way into that church at Corinth established by Paul, and it resulted in strife among the disciples. One
said, "I am of Apollos"; another, "I am of Cephas"; and another,
"I am of Paul." Paul saw that this biased strife and lack of love
among God's dear people would be disastrous to the church
and so he wrote this letter.

I've often said that if every true believer could move into
this chapter and live in the spirit of it for twelve months, the
church would double its numbers within that time. One of the
great obstacles in the way of God's work today is this lack of
love among the disciples of the Lord Jesus Christ.

If we love a person, we won't be pointing out his failings all
the time. It is said:

Many rules of eloquence have been set forth, but, strange,
to say, the first and most essential of all has been overlooked,
namely, love. To address people fittingly they must be loved
much. Whatever they may be, be they ever so guilty, or indifferent, or ungrateful, or however deeply sunk in crime, before

all, and above all, they must be loved. Love is the sap of the gospel, the secret of lively and effectual preaching, the power of eloquence. The goal of preaching is to reclaim the hearts of men for God, and nothing but love can find out the mysterious avenues which lead to the heart. If then you do not feel a fervent love and profound pity for humanity, be assured that the gift of Christian eloquence has been denied you. You will not win souls, neither will you acquire that most excellent of earthly sovereignties – sovereignty over human hearts. An Arab proverb runs thus – "The neck is bent by the sword, but heart is only bent by heart." Love is irresistible.[1]

> Love is the sap of the gospel, the secret of lively and effectual preaching, the power of eloquence.

Look at these words again: [Love] *suffers long and is benign;* [love] *envies not.* So often, if one person outshines another, it leads to envy in our hearts toward that one. We need a great deal of grace to keep it in check. [Love] *does nothing without due reason, is not puffed up.* One of the worst enemies Christians have to contend with is this spirit of rivalry – this feeling of, "Who shall be the greatest?" *Then there arose a dispute among them, which of them should be the greatest* (Luke 9:46).

Some years ago, I read a book that did me a great deal of good. It was titled *The Training of the Twelve.* The writer said that during the three years Christ was engaged publicly going about His Father's business, He spent most of His time training twelve men. The training He gave them was very different from the training of present-day schools. The world teaches men that they must seek to be great. Christ taught His disciples that they must be little – that in honor, they must prefer one another and are not to be puffed up. Nor are they to harbor

---

1   *The Homiletic Review,* Volume 20, Page 103.

feelings of envy, but are to be full of meekness, gentleness, and lowliness of heart.

When a well-known painter was asked to paint a perfect likeness of Alexander the Great, he found the request difficult. In war, Alexander had been struck by a sword which left an immense scar across his forehead. The painter said, "If I keep the scar, it will be an offense to the admirers of the monarch, and if I omit it, it will fail to be a perfect likeness. What shall I do?" He hit upon a happy, pragmatic solution. He represented the emperor leaning on his elbow, with his forefinger on his brow, accidentally, as it seemed, covering the scar on his forehead. Isn't it possible for us to represent each other with the finger of love on the scar, instead of representing the scar deeper and blacker than it really is? Christians can learn a lesson of charity – of human kindness and of love even from the nonbelieving world.

This spirit of seeking to be the greatest has nearly ruined the church at different times in history. If the church were not divine, it would have completely disintegrated long ago. Today, through this miserable spirit of ambition and self-seeking, there's hardly any movement of reform that hasn't been in danger of being thwarted and destroyed. May God empower us to get above this, to cast away our conceit and pride, and to accept Christ as our teacher so He can show us the spirit in which His work should be done.

One of the saddest things in the life of Christ was the working of this spirit of pride among His disciples, even in the last hours of His interaction with them, just before He was led away to be crucified. In Luke 22:21-27, we read: *But with all this, behold, the hand of him that betrays me is with me on the table. And truly the Son of man goes as it was determined; but woe unto that man by whom he is betrayed! And they began to enquire among themselves, which of them it was that should do this thing. And there was also a contention among them, which of them should be accounted the greatest. Then he said unto them, The kings of the Gentiles exercise lordship over them, and those that exercise authority upon them are called well-doers. But ye shall not be so, but he that is greatest among you, let him be as the younger; and he that is prince, as he that doth serve. For who is greater, he that sits at the table or he that serves? Is it not he that sits at the table? But I am among you as he that serves.*

Right there, on that memorable night, when Jesus instituted the Last Supper, after they'd eaten of the Passover lamb and the Savior was on His way to the cross – even there this spirit arose among them about who would be the greatest.

A charming tradition that is connected with the site on which the temple of Solomon was erected tells the tale of two brothers who were said to occupy the land at one time. One of the brothers had a family; the other had none. On this spot, a field of wheat was sown and on the evening following the harvest, the wheat had been gathered in separate shocks. The older brother said to his wife, "My younger brother is unable to bear the burden and heat of the day; I will arise, take from my shocks, and place them with his without his knowledge." The younger brother, being motivated by the same benevolent intentions, said to himself, "My elder brother has a family, and I have none. I will arise, take of my shocks, and place it with his."

Imagine their mutual astonishment when, on the following day, they found their respective shocks undiminished. This course of events transpired for several nights, when each of the brothers resolved to stand guard and solve the mystery. They did so on the following night and they met each other halfway between their respective shocks with their arms full. On ground sanctified by such associations as this, the temple of Solomon was erected – spacious and magnificent – to the wonder and admiration of the world. Sadly, these days, how many would sooner steal their brother's entire shock of grain than add a single sheaf to it?

If we want to be wise in winning souls and to be vessels for the Master's use, we must get rid of the accursed spirit of self-seeking. That is the purpose of this thirteenth chapter in Paul's first letter to the Corinthians. He told them that a man might be full of faith and zeal and that he might even be very kind, but if he didn't have love, he was like sounding brass and a tinkling cymbal. I believe many ministers might as well go into the pulpit and blow a tin horn Sunday after Sunday as to go on preaching without love. A man can preach the truth. He can be perfectly sound in doctrine, but if there is no love in his heart going out to those whom he addresses, and if he is doing it only professionally, the apostle says he is only sounding brass.

It isn't always *more* work that we need so much as *a better motive*. Many of us do a lot of work, but we must remember that God looks at the motive. The only tree on this earth that can produce fruit which is pleasing to God is the tree of love.

When writing to Titus, Paul says, *But speak thou the things which are expedient unto sound doctrine, that the aged men be temperate, venerable, prudent, sound in faith, in charity, in tolerance* (Titus 2:1-2). What good is a sermon, no matter how sound in doctrine, if it isn't delivered with love and in patience? What are our prayers worth without the spirit of love?

People ask, "Why isn't there a blessing? Our minister's sermons and prayers are very good." Most likely, you'll find it is because the whole thing is done professionally as a job. The words glisten like icicles in the sun, and they are just as cold. There's no spark of love in them. If that is the case, there will be very little power. You can have your prayer meetings, your praise meetings, your faith and hope meetings; you can *talk* about all these things, but if there is no love mingled with them, God says you are as sounding brass and a tinkling cymbal.

Now a man can be a very good doctor and yet have no love for his patients. He can be a very clever and successful lawyer and have no love for his clients. A merchant can prosper greatly in business without caring at all about his customers. A person can have the ability to explain the wonderful mysteries of science or theology without any love. But no one can be a true worker for God and a successful winner of souls without love. He can be a great preacher in the eyes of the world and have crowds flocking to hear him, but

> When we reach a higher plane of love, it won't be hard for us to work for the Lord.

if love of God and souls isn't the motivating power, the effects will all pass away like the morning cloud and early dew.

It is said that when the men of Athens went to hear Demosthenes speak they were genuinely stirred up, and felt they must go and fight Philip of Macedon. Another orator of that day might have carried them away by his eloquence, but when the oration was over, all the influence vanished. It was nothing but fine words.

A man can be very eloquent and use great flowing language – he can sway the multitudes while they are under his influence, but if there's no love behind what he says, it will all be for nothing. It was Demosthenes' love for his country that stirred him, and then he stirred the people.

When we reach a higher plane of love, it won't be hard for us to work for the Lord. We will be glad to do anything, however small. God hates the countless big things in which love is not the motivating power, but He delights in the little things prompted by love. A cup of cold water given to a disciple in the spirit of love is of far more value in God's sight than the taking of a kingdom done out of ambition and vainglory.

I'm getting sick and tired of hearing the word *duty*. You hear so many talk about it being their duty to do this or that. My experience is that such Christians have very little success. Isn't there a much higher platform than mere duty? Can't we engage in the service of Christ because we love Him? When that is the compelling power it is so easy to do the work. It isn't hard for a mother to watch over a sick child. She doesn't look at it as a hardship. You never hear Paul talking about what a hard time he had in his Master's service. He was compelled by his love of Christ and by the love of Christ to him. He counted it a joy to labor, and even to suffer, for his blessed Master. *Count it all joy when ye fall into diverse trials* (James 1:2).

Perhaps you're thinking I shouldn't speak against duty, because a good amount of work wouldn't get done at all if it wasn't done out of a sense of duty. But I want you to see what a poor, sad motive that is, and how you can reach a higher level of service.

I'm thinking of going back to my home soon. In my mind, I see my old, white-haired mother living on the banks of the Connecticut River in the same little town where she's lived for the last eighty years. Suppose when I return I take her some present, and when I give it to her, I say, "You have been so very kind to me in the past that I thought it was my duty to bring you a present." What would she think? The real question is, how is this different than if I told her I gave it to her simply because of my strong love for her? How much more would she value it? God also wants His children to serve Him because of something other than duty. He doesn't want us to feel it is difficult to do His will.

Take an army that fights because it is forced to do so. The soldiers won't gain many victories. But how different it is when they are full of love for their country and for their commanders. Then nothing can stand in their way. Don't think you can do any work for Christ and hope to succeed if you aren't driven by love.

Napoleon tried to establish a kingdom by the force of arms.

So did Alexander the Great, Caesar, and other great warriors, but they utterly failed. Jesus founded His kingdom on love, and it is going to stand. When we reach this level of love, then all selfish and unworthy motives will disappear, and our work will stand the fire when God puts it to the test.

Another thing I want you to bear in mind is that love never looks to see what it is going to get in return. In the gospel of Matthew, we read of the parable of the man who went out to hire laborers so he could send them to work in his vineyard. After he hired and sent out some in the morning, he found others standing idle later in the day. He sent them to work also. It so happened that those who went out last got back first. Those who went out early in the morning thought they would be rewarded with more wages than those who went to work at the eleventh hour. When they learned they were only to get the same amount of money, they began to murmur and complain. But what was the good man's answer? He answered one of them and said, *Friend, I do thee no wrong; didst not thou agree with me for a denarius? Take that which is thine and go, for I desire to give unto this last one, even as unto thee. Is it not lawful for me to do what I will with mine own? Is thine eye evil because I am good? So the first shall be last, and the last first* (Matthew 20:13-16).

I have generally found that those workers who are looking to see how much they are going to get from the Lord all the time are never satisfied. But love does its work and makes no bargain – no deal expecting something in return. Let us make no bargains with the Lord, but be ready to go out and do whatever He *hires* us to do.

I am sure if we go out cherishing love in our hearts for those we are going to try and reach, every barrier will be swept out of the way. Love results in love, just like hatred precipitates hatred. Love is the key to the human heart. Someone once said, "Light is for the mind, and love is for the heart." When you can reach men's hearts, then you can turn them toward Christ. But first, we must win them to ourselves.

You may have heard of the boy whose home was near the woods. One day he was in the woods, and he thought he heard the voice of another boy nearby. He shouted, "Hello there!" and the voice shouted back, "Hello there!" He didn't know it was the echo of his own voice, and he shouted again, "You are a mean boy!" Again, the cry came back, "You are a mean boy!" After more of the same, he went into the house and told his mother about the bad boy in the woods.

His mother, who understood what had happened, said to him, "Oh no! Speak kindly to him, and see if he doesn't speak kindly to you." He went to the woods again and shouted, "Hello there!" "Hello there!" came the reply. "You are a good boy." Of course, the reply came, "You are a good boy." "I love you." "I love you," said the other voice.

You smile at that, but this little story explains the secret of the whole thing. Some of you may think you have bad and disagreeable neighbors. If that's the case, it

Love is the key that will unlock every human heart.

is most likely that the trouble is with you. If you love your neighbors, they will love you. As I said before, love is the key that will unlock every human heart. No man or woman in all this land is so low and so degraded that you can't reach them with love, gentleness, and kindness. It may take years, but it can be done.

Love must be active. As someone has said, "A man can hoard up his money. He can bury his talents in a napkin, but there is one thing he can't hoard up – love." You can't bury it. It *must* flow out from us. It can't feed upon itself. It must have an object.

A few years ago, when we had yellow fever in one of the Southern cities, I read about a family that had just moved into an unfamiliar neighborhood. The father was stricken with the fever. There were so many fatal cases happening that the authorities didn't stop to give them a decent burial. The dead-cart went through the streets where the poor lived, and the bodies were carried away for burial.

The neighbors of this family were afraid. No one would visit the house because of the fever. It wasn't long before the mother was stricken with it too. Before she died, she called her boy to her and said, "I will soon be gone, but when I am dead, Jesus will come and take care of you." She had no one on earth to whom she could commit him. In a little while, she too was gone, and they carried her body away to the cemetery. Her young son followed her to the grave. He saw where they laid her, and then he came back to the house.

He found it very lonely, and when it grew dark, he became afraid and couldn't stay in the house. He went out and sat on the step and began to weep. Finally, he went back to the cemetery, and finding the lot where his mother was buried, he laid down and wept himself to sleep.

The next morning, a stranger passing that way found him on the grave still weeping. "What are you doing here, my boy?"

"Waiting for the Savior."

The man wanted to know what he meant, and the boy told the story of what his mother had said to him. It touched the heart of the stranger, and he said, "Well, my boy, Jesus has sent me to take care of you."

The boy looked up and replied, "You have been a long while coming."

If we have the love of our Master, are you telling me that these outlying masses wouldn't be reached? There isn't a drunkard who wouldn't be reached. There's not a poor fallen one, or a blasphemer, or an atheist, who wouldn't be influenced for good. Atheists can't get over the power of love. It will upset atheism and every false system quicker than anything else. Nothing will break the stubborn heart so quickly as the love of Christ.

I was in a certain home a few years ago where a boy lived who was treated like one of the family, and yet he didn't have the same name as the rest of the family. One night I asked the lady of the house to explain this to me. I said, "I have noticed that you treat him exactly like your own children, yet he is not your boy."

"Oh no," she said. "He isn't, but it's quite true I treat him as my own child."

She went on to tell me his father and mother were American missionaries in India. They had five children. The time came when the children had to be sent away from India, because they couldn't receive an education there. They were to be sent to America for that purpose. The father and mother had been blessed in India, but didn't feel as though they could give up their children. They thought they would leave their missionary work in the foreign field and go back to America.

Back in America, they weren't blessed to the same extent as they had been in India. The natives wrote to them asking them to return. After a time, they decided that the call to return to India was so loud that the father must go back. The mother said to him, "I can't let you go alone. I must go with you."

"But how can you leave the children?" he asked. "You have never been separated from them."

She said, "I can do it for Christ's sake." Thank God for such love as that.

When it became known that they wanted to leave their children in good homes, this lady with whom I was staying told the mother that if she left one of them with her she would treat the child as her own. The mother came and stayed a week in the house to see that everything was right. The last morning came. When the carriage drove up to the door the mother said, "I want to leave my boy without shedding a tear. I can't bear to have him think it costs me tears to do what God has for me to do."

My friend saw the great struggle going on, because she heard the mother crying in the adjoining room. The mother cried, "O God, give me strength for the hour. Help me now." She came downstairs with a beautiful smile on her face. She hugged her boy to her bosom, kissed him, and left him without a tear. She left all her children, and went back to work for Christ in India, and before very long, she left the shores of India to be with her Master in heaven. That is what a weak woman can do when love for Christ is the motivating force. Sometime after that, the dear boy passed away to be with the mother.

A few years ago, when preaching in a certain city, I found a young man very active in bringing boys from the street into the church meetings. If there was a difficult case in the city, he was sure to come across it. He could often be found in the inquiry room with a whole crowd around him. I became deeply interested in the young man and grew close to him. I learned he was another son of that same distinguished, glorious missionary. I found that all their sons were in training to go out as foreign missionaries, to take the place of the mother and father who had gone to their reward. It made such an impression on me that I couldn't shake it off. These boys have all gone out among the unbelieving heathen to tell the story of Christ and His love.

I am convinced of this: When these hard-hearted people who now reject the Savior are thoroughly awake to the fact that love is prompting our efforts on their behalf, the hardness will begin to soften, and their stubborn wills will begin to bend. This key of love will unlock their hearts. We can turn them, with God's help, from the darkness of this world to the light of the gospel. *For the God, who commanded the light to shine out of darkness, has shined in our hearts to bring forth the light of the knowledge of the clarity of God in the face of Jesus Christ* (2 Corinthians 4:6).

Christ gave His disciples a badge. Some of you wear a blue ribbon and others wear a red ribbon, but the badge that Christ gave to His disciples was love – love not only for those who are Christians, but love also for the fallen. The Good Samaritan had love for the poor man who had fallen among thieves. If we are filled with such love as that, the world will soon find out that we are the followers of the Lord Jesus Christ. *By this shall everyone know that ye are my disciples, if ye have love one to another* (John 13:35). It will do more to upset unfaithfulness and rebellion against God than anything else.

Speaking about difficult people being reached for Christ reminds me of a time I was in a home in London. A young lady in that home felt she wasn't doing as much for Christ as she would like and decided to start a class for boys. She now has fifteen to twenty of these lads, ranging from age thirteen to sixteen – a very difficult age to deal with. This Christian young lady made up her mind that she would first try and win the friendship of these boys for herself, and then seek to lead them to the Savior. It is a beautiful sight to see how she has won their young hearts for herself, and I believe she will win them all to a pure and godly life. If we are willing to work among the young with such a spirit, boys such as these will be saved. Instead of helping to fill our prisons and poorhouses, they will become useful members of God's church and a blessing to society.

I have a friend who has a large Sunday school. When he began, he made up his mind that if a boy didn't have good training in his own home, he couldn't get it anywhere but in Sunday school, and so he resolved that, if possible, when a boy was rebellious and headstrong he wouldn't turn him away purposeless.

One boy came to the school whom no teacher seemed able

to manage. One after another came to the superintendent and said, "You must take him out of my class. He's demoralizing all the others. He uses profane language and is doing more harm than all the good I can do."

Finally, my friend made up his mind that he would have the boy expelled publicly. He told a few of the teachers what he planned to do, but a wealthy young lady said, "I wish you would let me try with the boy. I will do all I can to win him."

My friend was sure she wouldn't have the patience needed to deal with him for very long, but he put the boy in her class as she requested. It didn't take long for the little fellow to break the rules in the class, and she corrected him. He got so angry that he lost his temper and spat in her face. She quietly took a handkerchief and wiped her face. At the close of the lesson, she asked him if he would walk home with her when school was over. "No," he said. "I don't want to speak to you." He finished by telling her that he wasn't coming back to that old school any more. She asked if he would let her walk along with him. Again, he said, "No.

She looked at him and said, "Well, I'm sorry you are going, but if you will call at my house on Tuesday morning and ring the front doorbell, there will be a small parcel waiting for you." She made it clear that she wouldn't be at home at the time, but if he asked the servant, he would receive it.

He replied, "You can keep your old parcel. I don't want it." However, she thought he would be there.

By Tuesday morning, the little fellow was over his mad fit, and he came to her house and rang the doorbell. The servant handed him the parcel. When he opened it, he found it contained a little vest, a necktie, and, best of all, a note written by the teacher. She told him how every night and every morning since he had been in her class she had prayed for him. Now that he was going to leave her, she wanted him to remember that as long as she lived she would pray for him, and she hoped he would grow up to be a good man.

The next morning the boy was in the drawing room waiting to see her before she came downstairs from her bedroom. When she did come down, she found him crying as if his heart would break. She kindly asked him what was wrong. "Oh," he said as he wiped the tears from his face. "I have had no peace since I got your letter. You have been so kind to me, and I have been so unkind to you. I wish you would forgive me."

Since then, my friend the superintendent has said, "There are about eighteen hundred children in the school, and there isn't a better boy among them."

Can't we do the same as that young lady did? Let us rededicate ourselves now to God and to His service.

Had I the tongues of Greeks and Jews,
    And nobler speech than angels use,
If love be absent, I am found,
    Like tinkling brass, an empty sound.

Were I inspired to preach and tell
    All that is done in heaven and hell;
Or could my faith the world remove,
    Still I am nothing without love.

Should I distribute all my store
    To feed the bowels of the poor;
Or give my body to the flame,
    To gain a martyr's glorious name,

If love to God, and love to men
    Be absent, all my hopes are vain;
Nor tongues, nor gifts, nor fiery zeal
    The work of love can e'er fulfill.

– Isaac Watts

Chapter 3

Faith and Courage

The crucial thing to note is that all our work for God should be faith in action. In all my life, I've never seen men or women disappointed in receiving answers to their prayers, if they are full of faith built on solid ground. *Therefore, whosoever hears these words of mine and does them, I will liken him unto a prudent man, who built his house upon the rock; and the rain descended, and the rivers came, and the winds blew and beat upon that house, and it did not fall, for it was founded upon a rock. And every one that hears these words of mine and does not do them shall be likened unto a foolish man, who built his house upon the sand; and the rain descended, and the rivers came, and the winds blew and beat upon that house, and it fell; and great was the fall of it* (Matthew 7:24-27). Of course, we must have assurance in Scripture for what we expect, but I'm sure we have that assurance when we come together to pray for a blessing on our friends and neighbors.

Unbelief is as much an enemy to the Christian as it is to the unconverted. It keeps back the blessing now as much as it did in the days of Christ. In the Bible, we read that in one place *he did not do many mighty works there because of their unbelief*

(Matthew 13:58). If Christ couldn't do this, how can we expect to accomplish anything if the people of God are unbelieving? I say that God's children alone are able to hinder God's work. Unbelievers, atheists, and sceptics can't do it. Where there is unity, strong faith, and expectation among Christians, a mighty work is always done.

In Hebrews, we read that without faith it is impossible to please God. *For he that comes to God must believe that he is and that he is a rewarder of those that diligently seek him* (Hebrews 11:6). This statement is addressed to people who are Christians as well as to those who are seeking God for the first time. All of us seek a blessing for our friends. We want God to revive us, but we also want the outlying masses to be reached. We read in this passage that God blesses those who *diligently seek him*. So let's *diligently seek him* today. Let us have great faith, and let our expectation be from God.

> I say that God's children alone are able to hinder God's work.

I remember when I was a boy, in the spring of the year when the snow melted away on the New England hills where I lived, I used to take a magnifying glass and hold it up to the warm rays of the sun. The rays struck it, and I could set the woods on fire. Faith is the magnifying glass that brings the fire of God out of heaven. It was faith that drew the fire down on Mount Carmel and burned up Elijah's offering. We have the same God today, and the same faith. Some people seem to think faith is getting old, and the Bible is out of date. But the Lord will revive His work, and we will be able to set the world on fire if each believer has a strong and simple faith.

In the eleventh chapter of the epistle to the Hebrews, the writer brings up one worthy person after another – each of them a man or woman of faith. They made the world better by living in it. Listen to this description of what was accomplished by these men and women of faith:

> *Who by faith won kingdoms, wrought righteous-*
> *ness, obtained promises, stopped the mouths of lions,*
> *quenched the violence of fire, escaped the edge of the*
> *sword, recovered from infirmities, were made valiant*
> *in battle, turned to flight the armies of foreign ene-*
> *mies; women received their dead raised to life again,*
> *and others were tortured, not accepting deliverance*
> *that they might obtain a better resurrection; and*
> *others experienced cruel mockings and scourgings,*
> *and added to this, bonds and imprisonment; they*
> *were stoned; they were sawn asunder, were tempted,*
> *were slain with the sword; they wandered about in*
> *sheepskins and goatskins; poor, afflicted, mistreated,*
> *(of whom the world was not worthy); they wandered*
> *in deserts and in mountains and in dens and caves*
> *of the earth. And these all, approved by testimony of*
> *faith, received not the promise, God having provided*
> *some better thing for us, that they without us should*
> *not be made perfect.* (Hebrews 11:33-40)

Surely, no child of God can read these words without being stirred. It is said that *women received their dead raised to life again.* Many of you have children who have gone far astray, taken captive by strong drink, or led away by their lusts and passions, and you've become really discouraged about them. But if you have faith in God, they can be raised up as from the dead and brought back again. The wanderers can be reclaimed. Drunkards and promiscuous women can be reached and saved. There is no man or woman, however low he or she may have sunk, who can't be reached.

In these times, we should have far more faith than Abel,

Enoch, or Abraham. They lived long ago on the other side of the cross. We talk about the faith of Elijah, the patriarchs, and the prophets, but they lived in the dim light of the past, while we are in the full blaze of Calvary and the resurrection. When we look back and think of what Christ did, how He poured out His blood so people could be saved, we should go forth in His strength and conquer the world. Our God is able to do great and mighty things.

Remember how the Roman centurion sent for Christ to heal his servant? When the Savior drew near, the centurion sent friends to Him to say that He need not take the trouble to come into his house. All that was needed was that He speak the word and his servant would live. He probably figured that if Christ had the power to create worlds, to say, *Let there be light* (Genesis 1:3), and there was light, and to make the sea and the earth bring forth abundantly, He could easily say the word and raise up his sick servant. We are told that when Christ received the Roman soldier's message He marveled at his faith. Let us have faith at this moment that God will do great things in our midst.

Caleb and Joshua were men of faith. They were worth more to Israel than all the camp of unbelievers and the other ten spies put together. We read that Moses sent out twelve men to spy out the land. Let me say that faith never sends out any spies. You may perhaps reply that Moses was commanded by God to send them out, but we read that it was because of the hardness of their hearts. If they had believed in God, they would have taken possession of the land at Kadesh Barnea. I suppose these twelve men were chosen because they were leading men and influential in the twelve tribes.

After they had been gone about thirty days, they came back with what we might call a minority and a majority report. All twelve admitted the land was a good land, but the ten said,

"We aren't able to take it. We saw giants there – the sons of Anak." Can't you just see these ten spies in camp the night they returned, with great crowds gathered around them listening to their negative reports, while very few probably gathered to hear Caleb and Joshua? It often seems people are much more ready to believe a lie than to believe the truth. As unbelieving men gathered around the ten spies, imagine one of them describing the giants in the land. "Why, I had to look all the way up in order to see their faces. The earth trembled as they walked. The mountains and valleys are full of them. Then we saw great walled cities. We aren't able to take the land."

But Caleb and Joshua had quite a different story to tell. Those mighty giants seemed to be like grasshoppers in their sight. These men of faith remembered how God had delivered them from the hand of Pharaoh and brought them through the Red Sea. They didn't forget how He had given them bread from heaven to eat and water to drink from the rock in the wilderness. If He marched with them, they believed they could go right up and take possession of the land. So they said, *Let us go up at once and possess it; for we are well able to overcome it* (Numbers 13:30).

What do we see in the church today? About ten out of every twelve professed Christians are looking at the giants, at the walls, and at the difficulties in the way. They say, "We aren't able to accomplish this work. We might be able to do it if there weren't so many bars and taverns – so much drunkenness – and so many atheists and opposers." Let's not give in to these unbelieving professors. If we have faith in God, we are perfectly able to go up and possess the land for Christ. God always delights to honor faith.

In the end, it could be that some godly frail woman, bedridden and unable to attend the meetings is found to have brought down the blessing. In the day when every person's work is tested, it might be revealed that some unknown person who honored God by a simple faith was the one who caused such a blessing to descend on our cities and shake things up.

Again, in these biblical accounts, we find faith is always followed by courage. Caleb and Joshua were full of courage, because they were men of faith. Throughout the ages, those who have been greatly used of God have been men of courage. If we are full of faith, we won't be full of fear and distrusting God all the time. That is the trouble with the church of Christ today – so many are fearful, because they don't believe God is going to use them. What we need is to have the courage that will compel us to move forward. If we do this, we may have to go against the advice of lukewarm Christians.

In biblical accounts, we find faith is always followed by courage.

Some people never seem to do anything but object or find fault, because the work isn't always carried out exactly as they see fit. They will say, "I don't think that's the best way to do things." When it comes to raising objections to any plans that can be suggested, they are very fruitful. If any step is taken to move forward, they are ready to throw cold water on it. They'll quickly point out all kinds of possible difficulties. We desire to have faith and courage which will enable us to move forward without waiting for these timid unbelievers.

In the second book of Chronicles, we read that King Asa had to go against his father and mother. It took a lot of courage to do that. He removed his mother from being queen and cut down the idols and burned them.

At times, we have to go against those who should be our best friends. Isn't it time for us to launch out into the deep? I've never seen people go out and try to bring people into the Lord's fold, except that the Lord gave His blessing. If a man has the courage to go straight to his neighbor and speak to him about his soul, God is sure to smile upon the effort. The person he speaks to may end up angry about it, but that isn't always a bad sign. Who knows, he may write a letter the next day and apologize. At any rate, it's better to make him angry in this way than for him to continue on to eternal death and ruin.

When God was about to deliver Israel out of the hand of the Midianites, notice how He taught this lesson to Gideon. Gideon had gathered an army of thirty-two thousand men. He probably counted them, and when he knew that the Midianites had an army of a hundred and thirty-five thousand, he said to himself, "My army is too small. I am afraid I won't succeed." But the Lord's thoughts were different. He said to Gideon, *The people that are with thee are too many* (Judges 7:2). So He told him that all those among the thirty-two thousand who were fearful and afraid should go back to their homes, to their wives and their mothers. No sooner had Gideon given this command than twenty-two thousand men stepped out of line and were sent home. Gideon could have thought the Lord had made a mistake as he watched his army melt away. If two-thirds of a big audience stood and walked out, you would think they were *all* going.

The Lord said, *The people are yet too many; bring them down unto the water, and I will try them for thee there; . . . Every one that laps of the water with his tongue as a dog laps, him shalt thou set by himself; likewise every one that bows down upon his knees to drink* (Judges 7:4-5). Again, he gave the word, and ninety-seven hundred wheeled out of line and went to the rear, so Gideon was left with three hundred men. But this handful of men whose hearts beat true to the God of heaven, and who were ready to go forward in His name, were worth more than all the others who were always sowing seeds of discontent and predicting defeat. Nothing will discourage an army like that, and nothing is more discouraging in a church than to have a number of the people expecting disaster all the time and saying things like, "We don't think this effort will amount to anything. It's not the way I think things should be done."

What would be good for the church is if all the fearful and faithless people were to step to the rear, and let those who are full of faith and courage take their empty pitchers and go forward against the enemy. This little band of three hundred men who were left with Gideon routed the Midianites, but it wasn't their own might that gave them the victory. It was *the sword of I AM The Hewer!* (Judges 7:20). If we go on in the name of the Lord, trusting His might, we will succeed.

Before Moses went up to heaven, he did all he could to encourage Joshua, to strengthen and praise him. There was no sign of jealousy in the heart of Moses, even though he wasn't allowed to go into the Promised Land. He went up to the top of Pisgah and saw that it was a good land, and he tried to encourage Joshua to go forward and take possession of it. After Moses was gone, we read that three times in one chapter God said to Joshua, "Be of good courage."

> *Be strong and of a good courage; for thou shalt*
> *cause this people to inherit the land as an inheri-*
> *tance, which I swore unto their fathers to give them.*
> *Only be thou strong and very courageous that thou*
> *mayest keep and do according to all the law, which*
> *Moses my slave commanded thee; turn not from*
> *it to the right hand or to the left that thou may be*
> *prospered in all the things that thou doest. This book*
> *of the law shall not depart out of thy mouth, but*
> *thou shalt meditate therein day and night that thou*
> *may keep and do according to all that is written*
> *therein; for then thou shalt make thy way to prosper,*
> *and then thou shalt understand everything. See that*

I command thee to be strong and of a good courage;
be not afraid, neither be thou dismayed; for I, the
LORD thy God, am with thee wherever thou goest.
(Joshua 1:6-9)

God cheered his servant. *No one shall be able to stand before thee*
all the days of thy life (Joshua 1:5). Soon after that, Joshua took
a walk around the walls of Jericho. As he walked around, he
saw a man standing before him with a
drawn sword in his hand. Joshua wasn't   **God uses those who**
afraid, but said, *Art thou one of us or*   **have courage and not**
one of our adversaries? (Joshua 5:13).   **those looking for defeat.**
His courage was rewarded, because the
man replied, *No, but I am the Prince of the host of the LORD*
(Joshua 5:14). He had been sent to encourage him and to lead
him on to victory.

So, you will find all through the Scriptures that God uses
those who have courage and not those looking for defeat.

Another thought: I never knew a case where God used a
discouraged man or woman to accomplish anything great for
Himself. Let a minister go into the pulpit in a discouraged
frame of mind and it becomes contagious. It soon reaches the
pews, and the whole church becomes discouraged. The same
is true with a Sunday school teacher. I never knew a worker
of any kind who was full of discouragement and successful in
the Lord's work. It seems God can't make use of such a person.

One man told me that he preached for a number of years
without any result. He used to say to his wife, as they went to
church, that he knew the people wouldn't believe anything
he said – and there was no blessing. This man had expected
nothing, and he received just what he expected. Finally, he saw
his mistake and asked God to help him. He took courage and
then the blessing came. *According to your faith be it unto you*

(Matthew 9:29). Dear friend, let's expect that God is going to use us. Let's have courage and go forward, looking to God to do great things.

Elijah on Mount Carmel was one man, and Elijah under the juniper tree was quite another man. In the one case, he was a giant and nothing could stand in his way. When he grew terrified at Jezebel's message, he lost heart and wished himself dead. God couldn't use him. The Lord had to go to him and say, *What doest thou here, Elijah?* (1 Kings 19:13). I wish God would speak to many professing Christians who are out of fellowship with Him, to show them they are of no use in His cause.

When Peter denied his Master, he was a very different man from what he was on the day of Pentecost. He had fallen out of fellowship with his Lord, and the words spoken by a servant nearly frightened him out of his life. He denied his Master with oaths and cursing. How terribly a man falls when he loses faith and courage.

> *Then they took him and led him and brought him into the house of the prince of the priests. And Peter followed afar off. And when they had kindled a fire in the midst of the hall and were set down together, Peter sat down among them. But a certain maid beheld him as he sat by the fire and earnestly looked upon him and said, This man was also with him. And he denied him, saying, Woman, I know him not. And after a little while another saw him and said, Thou art also of them. And Peter said, Man, I am not. And about the space of one hour after, another confidently affirmed, saying, Of a truth this fellow also was with him, for he is a Galilaean. And Peter said, Man, I know not what thou sayest. And immediately while he yet spoke, the cock crew. Then*

the Lord turned and looked upon Peter. And Peter
remembered the word of the Lord how he had said
unto him, Before the cock crows, thou shalt deny me
three times. And Peter went out and wept bitterly.
(Luke 22:54-62)

But he was restored. Look at him on the day of Pentecost. If that maid whose question made him tremble had been in the crowd and heard him preach the marvelous sermon recorded in Acts 2, I imagine she would have been the most amazed person in all Jerusalem. She probably would have said something like, "Why, I saw him a few days ago, and he was terribly distressed at being called a disciple of Christ. Now he stands up boldly for this same Christ. He has no shame now." God used Peter mightily on the day of Pentecost, as he preached to that vast crowd that even included some of the very murderers of his Lord and Master. But our Lord couldn't use Peter until he repented of his cowardice and had his faith and courage restored. Consequently, when a person working for Christ loses heart and gets discouraged, the Lord has to lay him aside.

A number of years ago, I became depressed for a good many weeks. One Sunday in particular, I preached and there didn't seem to be any result. On the following Monday, I was really down. I sat in my study looking at myself and brooding over my lack of success. A young man called on me, who had a Bible class of a hundred adults in the Sunday school which I managed. As he came in, I could see he was emotionally way up on the mountaintop, while I was down in the valley. He said, "What kind of a day did you have yesterday?"

"Very poor." I grumbled. "I had no success, and I feel quite miserable. How was your day?"

"Oh, I never had a better day."

"What was the subject of your lesson?"

"I spoke on the life and character of Noah. Did you ever preach on Noah? Did you ever study up on his life?"

"Well, no. I don't know that I ever did that particular study." I thought I knew pretty much all there was about him in the Bible – you know – all that is taught about him is contained in a few verses.

My young friend said, "If you never studied it before, you had better do it now. It will do you good. Noah was a wonderful character."

When the young man went out of my office, I took out my Bible and some other books, and read all I could find about Noah. I hadn't been reading long before the thought came stealing over me: *Here was a man who toiled for a hundred and twenty years and never had a single convert outside of his own family. Yet he did not get discouraged.* I closed my Bible. The cloud had gone. I started out by going to the noon prayer meeting. I hadn't been there long when a man got up and said he'd come from a little town in Illinois. On the day before, he had admitted a hundred young converts to church membership. As he spoke, I said to myself, "I wonder what Noah would have given if he could have heard that. He never had any such result as that for his efforts."

After a few minutes, a man who sat right behind me stood up. The man was trembling. His hand rested on the back of my seat, and I felt it shake. He said, "I wish you would pray for me. I would like to become a Christian." I thought, *I wonder what Noah would have given if he had heard that. He never heard a single soul asking God for mercy, yet he didn't get discouraged.* I have never let myself get depressed like that since that day. Let's ask God to take away the clouds of fear and unbelief. Let's get out of Doubting Castle. Let's move forward courageously in the name of our God and expect to see results.

If you can't engage actively in the work, you can do a good

deal by encouraging others. Some people not only do nothing to advance the work, but they also consistently throw discouragement on others, in every forward step they take. If you meet with them, they seem to chill you through and through. I think I'd rather face the east wind in Edinburgh in the month of March, than come in contact with some of these so-called Christians. Such people may say something about an effort like, "Well, yes, a good deal of work was done, but not many were reached at all." Then they go on to say that things ought to have been done in a different way, but they have no idea how. They look at the dark side all the time.

If we can't be in the battle, we must try to find ways to encourage those who are.

Don't listen to such gloomy, discouraging remarks. In the name of our great Commander, let's march on to battle and to victory. Some generals have names worth more than a whole army of ten thousand men. In our army in the Civil War, there were some whose presence cheered all the ranks. As they passed the line of soldiers, cheer upon cheer went up. The men knew who was going to lead them, and they were sure of success. "The boys" liked to fight under such generals.

Let's encourage ourselves in the Lord, and encourage each other. Then we will have good success.

In the book of 1 Chronicles, we see Joab encouraging those helping him in warfare. *Be of good courage, and let us behave ourselves valiantly for our people and for the cities of our God; and let the LORD do that which is good in his sight* (1 Chronicles 19:13). Let's go forward in this spirit, and the Lord will help us triumph over our enemies. If we can't be in the battle, we must try to find ways to encourage those who are.

A Highland Scottish chief of the MacGregor clan fell wounded at the battle of Sheriffmuir. Seeing their leader fall, the clan wavered and gave the enemy an advantage. The old chieftain perceived this and raised on his elbow while the blood streamed from his wounds. He cried out, "I am not dead, my children; I am looking at you to see you do your duty." This energized them and roused them to make an almost superhuman effort. When our strength fails and our hearts sink within us, the Captain of our salvation cries, *Observe all things whatsoever I have commanded you; and, behold, I am with you always even unto the end of the age* (Matthew 28:20). *Be thou faithful unto death, and I will give thee the crown of life* (Revelation 2:10).

A friend of mine told me about a worker who came to him very depressed. Everything was going wrong. My friend turned to him and said, "Do you have any doubt about how things will turn out in the end? Is Jesus Christ going to set up His kingdom and reign from the rivers to the ends of the earth? Is He going to triumph or not?"

The man said, "Of course Christ is going to triumph." But he admitted that he'd never thought of it in that light. If people would take a look into the future at times and remember the promises, they wouldn't be depressed.

Christ is going to reign, so let's go out and do the work He has given us to do. If things happen to be dark around us, let's remember it is light somewhere else. If we aren't succeeding as much as we would like, it may be that others are seeing more victorious results.

Think of the opportunities we have compared with the early Christians. Look at the mighty obstacles they encountered – how they often sealed their testimony with their blood. See what Peter had to fight against on the day of Pentecost, when the people looked on him with scorn. The disciples in those days had no team to put up large buildings in which they could preach. They had no group of ministers sitting nearby to pray for them or help cheer them on. Yet look at the wonderful results of Peter's preaching on the day of Pentecost.

Look at the dense darkness that surrounded Martin Luther in Germany. Look at the difficulties that John Knox met with in Scotland. Yet these men did a mighty and a lasting work for God in their day and generation. We reap the blessed fruits of their faithful labors even now. Look at the darkness that brooded over England in the days of Wesley and Whitefield. See how God blessed their efforts. Yet they faced a great many obstacles that we don't have today. They went forward with strong and courageous hearts, and the Lord gave them success.

I believe if our forefathers who lived in the last century could come back to this world in the flesh, they would be amazed to see the wonderful opportunities we have. We have a great many advantages they didn't possess and probably didn't even dream possible. We live in a grand and glorious day.

It took John Wesley months to cross the Atlantic. Now we can do it in days. Think of the power of the printing

God is ready and willing to work, if we are ready and willing to let Him and to be used by Him.

press. We can print and scatter sermons to the corners of the earth. Look at the marvelous conveniences we have like the electric telegraph, and the railway train, which makes it possible to go and preach hundreds of miles away in a few hours. Don't you agree that we live in a glorious day? So let's not be discouraged. Instead, let's use all these wonderful opportunities and honor God by expecting great things. If we do, we won't be disappointed. God is ready and willing to work, if we are ready and willing to let Him and to be used by Him.

Some who are old and feeble might be saying to themselves, "I wish I were young again. I would like to go out into the thick of the battle." But anyone, young or old, can go into the homes of people and invite them to come out to the meetings. There are large halls everywhere with plenty of room. Many are ready to help sing the gospel, and it will also be preached. Many who won't go to a regular place of worship might be persuaded to come to a revival meeting.

If you aren't able to go out and invite people, as I said earlier, you can still cheer on the ones doing the work and wish them success. Many times, when I've come down from the pulpit, some old man, trembling, on the very verge of death, and living perhaps on borrowed time, has caught hold of my hand, and in a quavering voice said, "God bless you!" How those words have cheered and helped me. So, if you are too feeble to do the work yourselves, many of you can speak a word of encouragement to your younger friends.

You can also pray. Pray that God will bless the words spoken and the efforts made. It is very easy to preach when others pray for you the whole time and are supportive of you, instead of criticizing and finding fault.

I suppose you've heard the story about the child who was rescued from the fourth floor of a house being engulfed by raging fire. The child came to the window as flames shot higher and higher. He cried out for help and a fireman started up the ladder of the fire escape to rescue the child. The wind swept the flames at him and it grew so hot that he wavered. It looked like he might have to return without the child. Thousands looked on, and their hearts shuddered at the thought of the child perishing in the fire if the fireman didn't reach him. Someone in the crowd cried, "Give him a cheer!" Cheer after cheer went up, and as the fireman heard them he gathered fresh courage. Up he went into the midst of the smoke and fire and brought the child down in safety. If you can't go and rescue the perishing yourself, you can at least pray for those who do, and cheer them on. If you do, the Lord will bless the effort.

Each one helped his neighbour; and each one said to his brother, Be of good courage. (Isaiah 41:6)

We are living, we are dwelling
    In a grand and awful time,
In an age on ages telling –
    To be living is sublime.

On! let all the soul within you
    For the truth's sake go abroad!
Strike! let every nerve and sinew
    Tell on ages – tell for God!

    – Cleveland Coxe

Chapter 4

Faith Rewarded

And it came to pass on a certain day, as he was teaching, that there were Pharisees and doctors of the law sitting by, who were come out of every town of Galilee and Judaea and Jerusalem; and the power of the Lord was present to heal them. And, behold, men brought in a bed a man who was paralyzed, and they sought means to bring him in and to lay him before him. And when they could not find any way they might bring him in because of the multitude, they went upon the housetop and let him down through the tiling with his couch into the midst before Jesus. And when he saw their faith, he said unto him, Man, thy sins are forgiven thee. (Luke 5:17-20)

Matthew, Mark, and Luke recorded this miracle. When any two or three of the gospel writers record a miracle, it is to bring out some important truth. It seems to me that the truth the Lord wants to teach us here is this: He placed worth on the faith of these four men who brought the paralyzed man to Jesus for healing. We aren't told whether the paralyzed man had any faith, but it was when Jesus saw *their* faith that His power went forth to cure the paralyzed man.

I want to say to all Christian workers, that if the Lord sees our faith for those whom we wish to be blessed, He will honor it. He has never disappointed the faith of any of His children yet. You can't find an instance in the Bible where any man or woman has exercised true faith in God and where it wasn't honored. Nothing the Savior found when He was on this sin-cursed earth pleased Him so much as to see the faith of His disciples. Nothing refreshed His heart so much.

We read in the gospel narrative that a great stir occurred in the town of Capernaum at this time. A few weeks before, the Savior had been thrown out of His native town of Nazareth. He had come down to Capernaum, and the whole country was greatly moved. His star was just rising, and His fame just beginning to spread to the public.

Peter's wife's mother had been healed by a word. The servant of an officer in the Roman army had been raised up from a sick bed, and the Savior had performed many other wonderful miracles. Men came to Capernaum from every town in Galilee and Judea and from Jerusalem. They had gathered to witness these wonderful events. The voice of John the Baptist rang through the land proclaiming that a prophet would soon make His appearance, whose shoestring he was not worthy to untie. While the Baptist proclaimed this message, the prophet Himself made His appearance in the northern part of the country, and all these wonderful things transpired.

The Pharisees and doctors of the law had come to Capernaum to look into the reports that were spreading. The house where they gathered was filled to overflowing, and these wise men were listening to the Savior's teaching. Many of them hardly believed a word He said, but there may have been some who believed among these wise men. Nicodemus and Joseph of Arimathea may have been there; if so, they weren't yet known as disciples of Jesus.

The writer of the gospel of Luke says, *the power of the Lord was present to heal them* (Luke 5:17). However, we aren't told that even one of them was healed. It is like this often now. The power of the Lord may be present to heal in these gatherings, yet many come and go without being healed of their spiritual diseases and wonder what it all means. What we need is to have the power of God in our midst.

A man came into one of our meetings in London. He found himself in a part of the hall where he couldn't hear a word of what was spoken or sung. He couldn't even hear the text or the portion of Scripture read. He sat through the service, so to speak, alone with his own thoughts. A little while later, he told someone that as he sat there, God had revealed Himself to him and spoke peace to his soul. It's possible for the power of God to be present to heal, even though someone can't hear the voice of their fellow man.

What we need is to have the power of God in our midst.

These four men in this gospel account were real workers. They were worth more than a houseful of these Pharisees and doctors of the law who came merely to look on and criticize. I don't know who the four men were, but I have always had great admiration for them. It may be that one of them had been blind and the Lord had given him sight. The other may have been lame from birth. When the Master restored this man to health he thought he would bring someone else to be healed. The third man may have been a cured leper, and he wished to help in getting some other afflicted person cured. Perhaps this paralyzed man was his next-door neighbor. The fourth man may have been deaf and dumb, and he thought he would use his newly acquired hearing and speech in helping someone else. These four young converts said, "Let's bring our sick neighbor to Christ." The paralyzed man may have said he had no faith in Christ, but these four friends may have told him how they had been cured, and if the Master could heal them, surely, He could heal a paralyzed man.

Now it seems to me nothing will wake up a man quicker than to have four people go after him in one day. People are sometimes afraid that they will encroach on each other's privacy if more than one worker happens to call at the same house. For my part, I wish every family had about forty invitations to each meeting.

Recently, I heard about a man, a non-churchgoer, who didn't believe in the Bible or religious things. Someone distributing tickets to an event asked him if he would go to the meetings. He grew quite angry. "No, I will not go. I don't believe in any of it at all, and won't be seen in such a crowd."

A second man came along, not knowing that anyone had talked to the unbelieving man standing before him. He also asked the man if he would accept a ticket for the meetings. The man was still angry and gave him a piece of his mind. He told him to keep his tickets.

Before long, a third man called on him and asked, "Would you take a ticket for these meetings?" By this time, the man was awakened spiritually, but still he declined the ticket.

He went into a shop to buy something, and the man in the shop put a ticket for the meetings into his package. When the customer arrived home and opened it, there he found a ticket. Finally, he got so excited that he went, not to our meeting, but to a neighboring church. I don't know if he has come to the Lord yet, but I believe he is in a hopeful condition.

If one visit to someone you want to reach doesn't wake them up spiritually, send a second visitor. If that has no effect, send a third, and a fourth, and a fifth, and a sixth, and a seventh. Go on like this day after day. It is a great thing to save one person, to get them out of the pit, to have their feet set fast on a rock and a new song put in their mouth. Nothing will rouse an indifferent man quicker than to have a number of friends go after him. If you can't bring him yourself, get others to help you.

These four men found an obstacle in the way. The door of the house was blocked, and they couldn't get their disabled friend near the Master. They may have asked some of these philosophers to stand aside, but no, they wouldn't do that. They wouldn't bother themselves for a sick man. Many people won't get into the kingdom of God themselves, and they throw obstacles in the way of others. After trying, probably for some time, to get in, these four men devised another plan. If it had been some of us, we most likely would have grown quite discouraged and carried the man back to his home.

These men had faith and perseverance too. They decided that somehow they were going to get their friend to Christ. If they couldn't get him through the door, they would find another way – through the roof. Some people might say, "Enthusiasm without knowledge." I'd rather have that than knowledge without enthusiasm. You can see them pulling and tugging away at the burden. If you have ever tried to carry a wounded man up a flight of stairs, you know it's not an easy matter. But these four men weren't going to be defeated, and they finally got him up on the roof.

This left them with one more question. "How can we get him down to where Jesus is?" They began to tear up the roof tiles. I can see those Pharisees and other wise men looking up and saying to one another, "What are those men doing? We've never seen anything like this in the temple or in any synagogue. It is altogether out of the ordinary. These men must be fanatics. Why, they've made a hole large enough for a man to fit through. Suppose a sudden rain shower were to come; it would damage the house."

But the four workers on the roof were extremely intense.

They let down the mat on which the man lay into the room. They situated their friend right at the feet of Jesus Christ. A good place to lay him, wasn't it? Perhaps you have a skeptical son or an unbelieving husband, or some other member of your family who scoffs at the Bible and sneers at Christianity. Lay them at the feet of Jesus, and He will honor your faith.

*When he saw **their** faith* (emphasis added). I suppose these men were staring down into the house to see what was about to take place. Christ looked up at them, and when He saw their faith He said to the paralyzed man, *Trust, son; thy sins are forgiven thee* (Matthew 9:2). That was more than they expected. They only thought of his body being made whole. Let's bring our friends to Christ, and we'll get more than we expect. The Lord met this man's deepest need first. It may be that his sins had brought on the paralysis, so the Lord forgave the man's sins first of all.

And the scribes and the Pharisees began to reason, saying, Who is this who speaks blasphemies? Who can forgive sins, but God alone? (Luke 5:21). The Master knew their thoughts and asked them, *What is easier, to say, Thy sins are forgiven thee, or to say, Rise up and walk? But that ye may know that the Son of man has power upon earth to forgive sins (he said unto the paralytic), I say unto thee, Arise and take up thy couch and go to thine house* (Luke 5:23-24). The man leaped to his feet made whole. He rolled up the old bed, swung it across his shoulders, and went to his house. Notice that the scribes and Pharisees who wouldn't make way to let him in now stood aside pretty quickly to let him go out. No need for him to go out by way of the roof; he went out through the door.

Fellow believer, let us have faith for those we bring to Christ. Let's believe for them, if they won't believe for themselves. There may be some who are reading this book who don't believe in the Bible, or in the gospel of the Son of God. Let us bring them to Christ in the arms of our faith. He is unchangeable – *the same yesterday and today and for the ages* (Hebrews 13:8). Let us look for great things to happen – to expect the dead to be raised, to reclaim women who prostitute their bodies, to see the drunkards saved and the devils cast out. I believe men are influenced by evil spirits, just like when the Son of God was on earth. We want to bring them right to the Lord Jesus Christ so He can heal and save them. Let this cursed unbelief be swept out of the way, and let us come to God as one, looking for and expecting signs and wonders to

He can perform miracles today, and He will if we ask Him to fulfill His promises.

be done in the name of Jesus. He can perform miracles today, and He will if we ask Him to fulfill His promises. *He is able also to save to the uttermost* (Hebrews 7:25).

To anyone unsaved reading this book, let me say that God has the power to save you from your sins today. If you want to be made new, come right to the Master as the leper did in Mark 1:40. He said, *If thou wilt, thou canst make me clean.* Christ honored his faith and said, *I will; be thou clean* (Mark 1:41). Notice that the man put "if" in the right place. *If Thou wilt.* He didn't doubt the power of the Son of God, but firmly stated that if Christ wanted to, He had all power needed to heal.

In comparison, the father who brought his son to Christ said, *If thou canst do any thing, help us, having mercy on us* (Mark 9:22), and the Lord straightened out his theology then and there. ***If thou canst believe** this, all things are possible to him that believes* (Mark 9:23, emphasis added). To the mothers reading this, can you believe for your boy? If you can, the Lord will speak the word, and it will be done.

It is good for us to get right down at the feet of the Master, like the poor woman who went to Elisha and told him about her dead child. He asked his servant to take his staff and lay it upon the dead child. But the mother wouldn't leave the prophet, even though he wanted her to go with the servant. She wasn't satisfied with the prophet's staff, or even with his servant. She wanted the master himself. So Elisha went with her, and it was a good thing he did, because the servant couldn't raise the child, but Elisha did.

We want to get beyond the staff and beyond the servant, right to the heart of the Master Himself. Let's bring our paralyzed friends to Him. It is said of Christ that in one place *he did not do many mighty works there because of their unbelief* (Matthew 13:58). Let's ask Him to take away our cursed unbelief, which hinders the blessing from coming down, and prevents those who are sick of the paralysis of sin from being saved.

> The faith that works by love,
>   And purifies the heart,
> A foretaste of the joys above
>   To mortals can impart:
>
> It bears us through this earthly strife,
>   And triumphs in immortal life.[2]

---

2   Lowell Mason, Edwards A. Park, and Austin Phelps, eds., *The Sabbath Hymn Book: For The Service of Song in the House of the Lord: Hymn 757, "Faith Which Worketh by Love"* (New York: Mason Brothers, 1859).

Chapter 5

Enthusiasm

*A*wake thou that sleepest and arise from the dead, and the Christ shall shine upon thee (Ephesians 5:14). I want to apply these words to the children of God. If the lost are to be reached by the gospel of the Son of God, Christianity must be more aggressive than it has been in the past. Christians have been on the defensive long enough. The time has come for us to enter a war of aggression. When we as children of God wake up and go to work in the vineyard, those living in wickedness all around us will be reached, but not in any other way. You can go to crowded meetings and discuss "How to reach the masses," but when you finish with the discussion, you have to put forth personal effort and actually do what you've discussed. Every man and woman who loves the Lord Jesus Christ must wake up to the fact that he or she has a mission in the world in this work of reaching the lost.

A man can talk in his sleep, and it seems to me that there is a good deal of that kind of thing going on in the Lord's work. A man can even preach in his sleep. A friend of mine sat up in his bed one night and preached a sermon right through. He was sound asleep the whole time. Next morning, his wife told him all about it, and he preached the same sermon in his church the next Sunday morning. I have a copy of it in print, and it's a good sermon. So, a man is able to not only talk but actually also preach in his sleep. I think many preachers today are fast asleep.

One thing we must remember is that a man can't *work* in his sleep. There is no better way to wake up a church than to put it to work. One man will wake up another in waking himself up. Of course, the moment we begin to work aggressively and declare war with the world, the flesh, and the Devil, someone who talks like they have a lot of experience will shake their head, and there will be an outcry of, *Zeal of God, but not according to knowledge* (Romans 10:2).

God calls those who are active and earnest – not lazy or idle.

I've heard this objection ever since I began the Christian life. Someone speaking the other day about work to be done said he hoped zeal would be tempered with moderation. Another friend wisely replied that he hoped moderation would be tempered with zeal. If that was always the case, Christianity would be like a red-hot ball rolling over the face of the earth. No power on earth can stand before the onward march of God's people when they are deeply sincere in accomplishing God's work.

In all ages, God has used those who were sincere and strongly motivated. Satan always calls idle men into his service. God calls those who are active and earnest – not lazy or idle. When we are thoroughly aroused and ready for His work, then He will gather us and use us.

Remember where Elijah found Elisha? He was ploughing in the field; he was at work. Gideon was at the threshing floor. Moses was away in Horeb looking after the sheep. None of these eminent servants of God were lazy or idle. What they did, they did with all their might. We need such men and women nowadays. Even if we don't have all the knowledge we would like to have, let us do the work with all the zeal God has given us.

Jeremy Taylor says:

> The zeal of the apostles was this, they preached publicly and privately, they prayed for all men, they wept to God for the hardness of men's hearts, they "became all things to all men, that they might gain some," they travelled through deeps and deserts, they endured the heat of the Sirian star and the violence of Euroclydon, winds and tempests, seas and prisons, mockings and scourgings, fastings and poverty, labour and watching, they endured every man and wronged no man, they would do any good thing and suffer any evil, if they had but hopes to prevail upon a soul; they persuaded men meekly, they entreated them humbly, they convinced them powerfully, they watched for their good, but meddled not with their interest; and this is the christian zeal, the zeal of meekness, the zeal of charity, the zeal of patience.

Many people are afraid of the word *enthusiasm*. Do you know what the original meaning of this word is? It means "in God." The person who is "in God" will surely be fired up with enthusiasm. When a man goes in to work filled with fire and zeal, he will generally overcome all opposition before him. In the army, a general who is full of enthusiasm will fire up his men and will accomplish a great deal more than one who is not stirred with the same spirit. Some people say that if we go on in this way, many mistakes will be made, and there probably will be. You never saw any boy learning a trade who didn't make a good many mistakes. If you don't go to work because you are afraid of making mistakes, you will probably make one great mistake

– the greatest mistake of your life – that of doing nothing. If we all do what we can, then much will be accomplished.

How often do we find Sunday school teachers doing their work without any enthusiasm? I have known a lot of wooden-like teachers. If I were a carpenter, I could manufacture any quantity of them. They have no heart, no fire, and no enthusiasm. Such a teacher comes into the classroom a few minutes after the appointed time. He sits down without speaking a word to any of the students, until the time comes for the lessons to begin. At the time the superintendent sets to begin, the teacher brings out a question book. He hasn't troubled himself to study the subject, so he brings out what someone else has written about it. Along with the question book, he also has an answer book.

Such a teacher will pick up the question book and ask, "John, who was the first man?" He glances at the book and says to himself, *Yes, that is the right question.*

John replies, "Adam."

Looking at the answer book the teacher says, "Yes, that is right." He looks again at the question book and asks, "Charles, who was Lot?"

"Abraham's nephew."

"Yes, my boy, that is right." And so he goes on. You may say that this is an exaggerated description, and of course, I don't mean to suggest it is literally true, but the picture isn't so exaggerated as you would suppose. Do you think a class of boys full of life and fire is going to be reached in that way with such an approach?

I like to see a teacher come into the class and shake hands with the students all around. "Johnnie, how do you do? Charlie, I am glad to see you. How's the baby? How's your mother? How are all the folks at home?" That is the kind of a teacher I like to see. When he begins to open up the lesson, all the students are interested in what he is going to say. He will be able to gain the attention of the whole class and to train them for God and for eternity. You can't find a person in the world who has been greatly used of God who hasn't been full of enthusiasm. When we go to work in this spirit, our work will begin to prosper, and God will give us success.

As I prepared to leave New York to go to England in 1867, a friend said to me, "I hope you go to Edinburgh to attend the general assembly this year. When I was there a year ago, I heard a speech I will never forget. Dr. Duff's speech set me all on fire for the Lord. I will never forget the hour I spent in that meeting."

Shortly after reaching England, I went to Edinburgh and spent a week there, in hopes that I might hear Dr. Duff speak. I went to work to find the narrative of the speech my friend referred to, and it stirred me wonderfully. Dr. Alexander Duff had been in India as a missionary for twenty-five years preaching the gospel and establishing schools. He came back with his vitality, health, and strength broken down. He was allowed to address the general assembly in order to make an appeal for men to go into the mission field. After he spoke for a considerable time, he became exhausted and fainted. They carried him out of the hall into another room. The doctors worked over him for some time until he finally began to recover. When he realized where he was, he roused himself and said, "I didn't finish my speech; carry me back and let me finish it." They told him that if he did that he would risk his life. Said he, "I will do it even if I die." So they took him back to the hall. My friend said it was one of the most solemn scenes he ever witnessed in his life.

They brought the white-haired man into the assembly hall. As he appeared at the door, every person sprang to their feet. Tears flowed freely as they looked on the grand old veteran. With a trembling voice, he said, "Fathers and mothers of Scotland, is it true that you have no more sons to send to India to work for the Lord Jesus Christ? The call for help is growing louder and louder, but few are coming forward to answer it. You have the money put away in the bank, but where are the laborers who will go into the field? When Queen Victoria wants men to volunteer for her army in India, you freely give your sons. You don't talk about them getting sick or about the demanding climate. But when the Lord Jesus calls for laborers, Scotland is saying, 'We have no more sons to give.'"

Turning to the president of the assembly he said, "Mr. Moderator, if it is true that Scotland has no more sons to give to the service of the Lord Jesus Christ in India, although I have lost my health in that land, if there are none willing to go and tell those heathen of Christ, then I will be off tomorrow, to let them know that there is one old Scotchman who is ready to die for them. I will go back to the shores of the Ganges and lay down my life as a witness for the Son of God."

> We want men today who are willing, if need be, to lay down their lives for the Son of God.

Thank God for such a man. We want men today who are willing, if need be, to lay down their lives for the Son of God. Then we will be able to make an impression upon the world. When they see we are serious, their hearts will be touched, and we will be able to lead them to the Lord Jesus Christ.

I didn't agree with Giuseppe Garibaldi's judgment in everything, but I must confess I admired his enthusiasm. I never saw his name in the papers or in a book, but I read all I could find about him. Something about him fired me up. I remember reading about the time when he was on the way to Rome in 1867 and was thrown into prison. I read the letter he sent to his companions. "If fifty Garibaldis are thrown into prison, let Rome be free." He didn't care about his own comfort, so long as the cause of freedom in Italy was advanced. If we have a love like this for our Master and His cause, so that we are ready to go out and do His work whatever it may cost us personally, you can count on it that the Lord will use us to build up His kingdom.

I have read about a man in the ninth century who came up against a king. The king had a force of thirty thousand men, and when he heard that this general had only five hundred men, he sent him a message that if he would surrender, he would treat him and his followers mercifully. Turning to one of his followers, the man said, "Take that dagger and drive it into your heart." The man at once pressed the weapon to his bosom and fell dead at the feet of his commander. Turning to another, he said, "Leap into that chasm over there." The man jumped into the jaws of death. When they looked down, they saw him dashed to pieces at the bottom. Then, turning to the king's messenger, the man said, "Go back to your king and tell him that I have five hundred such men. Tell him we may die but we will never surrender. Tell him that I will have him chained with my dogs within forty-eight hours."

When the king heard this reply, he organized his men against him, but it struck terror in the king's heart. His forces were so demoralized they scattered like chaff before the wind. Within forty-eight hours, the king was taken captive and chained with the dogs of his conqueror. When the people see that we are serious in all we undertake for God, they will begin to tremble. Men and women will be asking about the way to Zion.

A fearful storm raged when the cry "Man overboard!" was heard. A human form was seen bravely opposing the furious elements in the direction of the shore, but the raging waves carried the struggler farther out rapidly, and, before the boats could be lowered, a fearful amount of space separated the victim from help. Above the shriek of the storm and the roar of the waters rose his rending cry. It was an agonizing moment. With bated breath and paled faces, every eye strained to see the struggling man. The rowers courageously strained every nerve in that race of mercy, but all their efforts were in vain. One wild shriek of despair and the victim went down. A piercing cry rang out through the hushed crowd. "Save him! Save him!" Into their midst an agitated man darted, throwing his arms wildly in the air shouting, "A thousand pounds for the man who saves his life!" But as he stared out, his eye rested only on the spot where the waves rolled remorselessly over the perished. He whose strong cry broke the stillness of the crowd was captain of the ship from whence the drowned man fell and was *his brother.* This is the feeling we want to have in the various ranks of those commissioned under the great Captain of our salvation. "Save him! He is my brother!"

The fact is men don't believe in Christianity because they think we aren't serious about it. In this same epistle to the Corinthians the apostle Paul says, *Ye are our epistle written in our hearts, known and read of all men* (2 Corinthians 3:2). I've never known a time when Christian people were ready to go forth and put in the sickle, that there wasn't a great harvest. Wherever you put in the sickle you'll find the fields ripe for harvest. *The harvest truly is great, but the labourers are few; pray ye therefore the Lord of the harvest that he would send forth labourers into his harvest* (Luke 10:2). The trouble is there are so few reapers to do the work.

God needs men and women. That's something far better than institutions. If a man or a woman is really serious, they won't wait to be put on some committee. If I saw a man fall into the river in danger of drowning, I wouldn't wait until I was placed on some committee before I tried to save him. Many people say they can't work for the Lord because they haven't been formally appointed. They say, "It isn't my parish."

I asked a person one day, during our last visit to London, if he would go and work in the inquiry room. He said, "I don't belong to this part of London." Let's look at the whole world as our parish, as a great harvest field. If God puts anyone within our influence, let's tell them about Christ and heaven. The world may rise up and say we are mad, but in my opinion no one is fit for God's service until he is willing to be considered mad by the world. They said Paul was mad. I wish we had many more who were bitten with the same kind of madness. As someone has said, "If we are mad, we have a good Keeper on the way and a good asylum at the end of the road."

One big problem is that people come to special revival meetings for two or three weeks and keep the fire stoked, but eventually it dies out. They are like a bundle of shavings with kerosene poured on them – they blaze away for a short time, but soon nothing is left. We need to keep the fiery fervor all the time – morning, noon, and night.

Don't be satisfied with merely pointing the children to the Lord Jesus Christ.

I heard about a well once that was said to be very good, except that it had two faults. It would freeze up in the winter, and it would dry up in the summer. A most extraordinary well, but I'm afraid there are a great number like it.

Many people are good at certain times. It might be better to say that they seem to be good "in spots." What we need is to be red hot all the time. Don't wait until someone seeks you out. People talk about striking while the iron is hot. I believe it was Oliver Cromwell who said, "Not only strike while the iron is hot, but make it hot by striking." So, let's stay vigilant at our post, and we'll soon grow warm in the Lord's work.

Let me say a few words especially for Sunday school teachers. I urge you. Don't be satisfied with merely pointing the children to the Lord Jesus Christ. Many teachers go on sowing the seed and think they will eventually reap the harvest, but they don't look for the harvest now. I began to work in that way, and it was years before I saw any conversions. I believe God's method is that we should sow with one hand and reap with the other. The two should go on side by side.

The idea that children must grow into manhood and womanhood before they can be brought to Jesus Christ is a false one. They can be led to Christ now in their youth, and they can be retained for the future when they can become useful members of society and a blessing to their parents, to the church, and to the world. If they are allowed to grow to maturity before they are led to Christ, many of them will be dragged into dens of vice, and instead of being a blessing they will be a curse to society.

What's the problem throughout Christendom today in connection with Sunday school? It is that so many drop through the Sunday school net when they grow up to the age of sixteen or so, and that's the last we see of them. Many young men who were once Sunday school students are now in our prisons. The cause of that is that so few teachers believe the children can be converted when they are young. They don't work to bring them to a knowledge of Christ, but are content only to go on sowing the seed. Let a teacher resolve that with God's help, he won't rest until he sees his whole class brought into the kingdom of God. If he determines to do this, he will see signs and wonders inside of thirty days.

> Let a teacher resolve that with God's help, he won't rest until he sees his whole class brought into the kingdom of God.

I remember clearly how I became aware of this. I had a large Sunday school with a thousand children. I was very pleased with the numbers. If we kept up or exceeded that number, I was delighted. If attendance fell below a thousand, it troubled me very much. I was simply aiming at numbers all the time. One class held in a corner of the large hall was made up of young women, and it was more trouble than any other in the school. Only one man could manage to keep it in order. If he could keep the class quiet, it was about as much as we could hope for. The idea of any of them being converted never entered my mind.

One Sunday this teacher was absent and his substitute struggled to keep order in the class. During the week, the teacher came to see me where I worked. He looked very pale, and I asked what was the trouble. "I have bleeding in my lungs," he said, "and the doctor tells me I won't live. I must give up my class and go back to my widowed mother in New York state." As he spoke, his chin quivered and the tears began to flow. He fully believed he was going home to die.

I said, "You're not afraid of death, are you?"

"Oh no, I am not afraid to die, but I will meet God and not one of my Sunday school students is converted. What will I say?"

How different things looked when he felt he was going to give an account of his stewardship.

I was speechless. I'd never heard anyone talk like this. I said, "Suppose we go and see the students and tell them about Christ."

"I'm very weak," he said. "Too weak to walk."

I took him in a carriage, and we went to the homes of every student. He staggered across the sidewalk, sometimes leaning on my arm. He called each young lady by name, prayed with her, and pleaded with her to come to Christ. It was a new experience for me, and it gave me a new perspective on things. After he had used up all his strength, I took him home. The next day he visited others in the class. Sometimes he went alone and sometimes I joined him. At the end of ten days, he came to see me where I worked with his face beaming with joy. He said, "The last one has yielded her heart to Christ. I am going home now. I have done all I can do. My work is done."

I asked when he was going. He said, "Tomorrow night."

"Suppose I ask these young friends to have a little gathering, to meet you once more before you go?"

He liked the idea, and so I sent out the invitations and they all came together. I had never spent such a night up to that time. I had never met such a large number of young converts, led to Christ by his influence and mine. We prayed for each member of the class, for the superintendent, and for the teacher. Every one of them prayed. What a change had come over them in a short space of time. We tried to sing, but that didn't turn out very well.

> Blest be the tie that binds
> Our hearts in Christian love.

We all said good-bye to him, but I felt as if I must go and see him once more. The next night, before the train left, I went to the station and found that, without any preplanning, one and another of the class came to say good-bye to him. They were all there on the platform. A few gathered around us – the fireman, engineer, brakeman, and conductor of the train, with the passengers. It was a beautiful summer night, and the sun was just going down behind the western prairies as we sang together:

> Here we meet to part again,
> But when we meet on Canaan's shore
> There'll be no parting there.

As the train pulled out of the station, he stood on the outside platform, and, with his finger pointing heavenward, he said, "I will meet you yonder." Then he disappeared from our view. What a work was accomplished in those ten days. Some of the members of that class were among the most active Christians we had in the school for years. Some of them are active workers today. A few years ago, I met one of them at work way out on the Pacific Coast.

We had a blessed work of grace in the school that summer. It took me away from my job and sent me into the Lord's work. If it hadn't been for the work of those ten days, I probably wouldn't be an evangelist today.

Let me urge Sunday school teachers, again, to seek the salvation of your students. Make up your mind that within the next ten days you will do all you can to lead your class to Christ.

Fathers and mothers, don't rest until you see all your family brought into the kingdom of God. Don't say He won't bless such a devoted effort. What we want today is the spirit of blessing and sanctification. May God pour out His Spirit upon us, and fill us with a holy enthusiasm.

Chapter 6

The Power of Little Things

I n Exodus 25:1-9 we read: *And the LORD spoke unto Moses,
saying, Speak unto the sons of Israel that they bring me an
offering; of every man that gives it willingly with his heart ye
shall take my offering. And this shall be the offering which ye
shall take of them: gold and silver and brass and blue and purple
and scarlet and fine linen and goats' hair and rams' skins dyed
red and badgers' skins and cedar wood, oil for the light, spices
for the anointing oil and for the sweet incense, onyx stones and
stones to be set in the ephod and in the pectoral. And let them
make me a sanctuary, that I may dwell among them. According
to all that I show thee, after the pattern of the tabernacle and the
pattern of all its vessels, even so shall ye make it.*

I'm glad this has been recorded for our instruction. It should
encourage us all to believe we can each have a part in building
up the walls of the heavenly Zion. In all ages, God has delighted
to use weak things. In 1 Corinthians 1:27-29, Paul speaks of
five things God uses: *God has chosen that which is the foolish-
ness of the world to confound the wise, and God has chosen that
which is the weakness of the world to put to shame the things
which are mighty; and that which is vile of the world and that*

which is despised God has chosen, and things which are not, to bring to nought the things that are, that no flesh should glory in his presence.

Notice the five things mentioned. God uses foolish things, weak things, base things, despised things, and things which are not. What for? *That no flesh should glory in his presence.* When

This world isn't going to be reached by mere human intellectual power.

we are weak then we are strong. People often think they don't have strength enough. The fact is, we have too much strength. It is when we feel we have no strength of our own, that we are willing for God to use us and work through us. If we are leaning on God's strength, we have more than all the strength of the world.

This world isn't going to be reached by mere human intellectual power. When we realize we have no strength, all the fullness of God will flow in on us. Then we will have power with God and with people.

In Revelation, we read that John wept at a sight he beheld in heaven. He saw a sealed book and *no one was found worthy to open the book nor to read it neither to look upon it* (Revelation 5:4). Abel, that holy man of God, wasn't worthy to open it. Enoch, who had been translated to heaven without tasting death, wasn't worthy. Elijah, who went up in a chariot of fire, and even Moses, that great lawgiver, or Isaiah, or any of the prophets – none was found worthy to open the book. As he saw this, John wept much. As he wept, someone touched him and said, *Weep not: behold, the Lion of the tribe of Juda, the Root of David, who has overcome to open the book and to loose its seven seals* (Revelation 5:5). When he looked to see who this Lion of the tribe of Judah was, whom did he see? The Lion was a Lamb! God's Lion is a Lamb! When we are like lambs, God can use us, and we are strong in His service. We can all be weak, can't we? Then let's lean on the mighty power of God.

All the men Christ called around Him were weak men in a worldly sense. They were all men without rank, without title, without position, without wealth or culture. Nearly all of them were fishermen and uneducated men, yet Christ chose them to build His kingdom. When God wanted to bring the children of Israel out of bondage, He didn't send an army. He sent one solitary man. So, in all ages, God has used the weak things of the world to accomplish His purposes.

I read about an incident some time ago that illustrates the power of a simple tract. It talked about a society established to distribute tracts by mail in the higher circles of society. One of these tracts, titled *Prepare to meet thy God*, was enclosed in an envelope and sent by post to a gentleman well known for his ungodly life and his reckless sinfulness. He was in his study when he read this letter among others. When he saw it, he said, "What's that, 'Prepare to meet thy God'? Who had the nerve to send me this hypocritical and sanctimonious jargon?" And, with a curse word toward his unknown correspondent, he arose to put the paper in the fire. But then he paused. "No, I won't do that," he said to himself. "On second thought, I know what I will do. I'll send it to my friend B—. It will be a good joke to hear what he'll say about it." So he enclosed the tract in a fresh envelope, and, in a fake handwriting different than his own, he directed it to his companion who lived much the same as him.

When Mr. B— received the tract, he cursed just like his friend, and his first impulse was to tear it in pieces. But then he thought, "I'll not tear it." The title, *Prepare to meet thy God*, grabbed his attention immediately and pierced his conscience. The arrow of conviction entered his heart as he read, and he was converted. One of his first thoughts was for the ungodly people he knew. "I've received such blessed light and truth; shouldn't I do my best to share it with others?" He folded the tract and enclosed it in an envelope and directed it to one of his companions in sin. Wonderful to say, the little arrow hit the mark, again. His friend read it and was also converted. Now both of them walked as the Lord's redeemed.

In Matthew 25:14-15 we read that the kingdom of heaven *is like a man travelling into a far country, who called his own slaves and delivered unto them his goods. And unto one he gave five talents, to another two, and to another one, to each one according to his faculty, and straightway took his journey.*

Note that he gave every man *according to his faculty.* He gave each servant just the number of talents he could care for and use. Some people complain they don't have any talents, but we each have the number of talents we can properly employ. If we take good care of what we have, God will give us more. Eight talents were distributed among three people. The master gave to one five, two to a second, and one to the third. The man went away on his journey, and the servants fully understood he expected them to improve their talents and trade with them. God isn't unreasonable. He doesn't ask us to do what we can't do, but He gives to us according to our peculiar capabilities, and He expects us to use the talents we have.

As we continue in the passage, we read:

> *He that had received five talents came and brought another five talents, saying, Lord, thou didst deliver unto me five talents; behold, I have gained beside them five talents more. His lord said unto him, Well done, thou good and faithful slave; thou hast been faithful over a few things; I will set thee over many things; enter thou into the joy of thy lord. He also that had received two talents came and said, Lord, thou didst deliver unto me two talents; behold, I have gained two other talents beside them. His lord said unto him, Well done, good and faithful slave;*

thou hast been faithful over a few things; I will set thee over many things; enter thou into the joy of thy lord (Matthew 25:20-23).

The one who had only two talents also doubled them, and so he had four talents. To him also, the Lord said, *Well done, good and faithful slave; . . . enter thou into the joy of thy lord.*

If the man who had the one talent had traded with it, he would have received exactly the same approval as the others. But what did he do? He put it into a napkin and buried it. This is how he thought he would take care of it.

After the lord of these servants had been gone a long time, he returned to compare accounts with them. What does he find in the case of the third servant? He has the one talent, but that's all.

I read about a man who had a thousand dollars. He hid it away, thinking he would take care of it in that way so that when he was an old man he would have something to fall back upon. After keeping the money for twenty years, he took it to a bank and got just one thousand dollars for it. If he had put it in an interest-bearing account, in the usual way, he might have had three times the amount. He made the mistake that a great many people make today throughout Christendom, of not trading with their talents. My experience, as I've gone about in the world and mingled with professing Christians, has been that those who find the most fault with others are those who have nothing to do. If a person is busy improving the talents God has given him, he will have too much to do to find fault and complain about others.

God has given us many opportunities for serving Him, and He expects us to use them. I've frequently heard people say, "I have a right to do what I want with my own," because people think their time and property are their own.

On one occasion, a friend stood beside the bed of a dying

military man who had held an important command in the successful Indian wars. He asked him if he was afraid to die. He instantly answered, "I am not. I have never done any harm."

The other replied, "If you were going to be tried by a court-martial as an officer and a gentleman, I suppose you would expect an honorable acquittal?" The dying old man lifted himself up and with his frail, limited energy, exclaimed, "That I would."

"But you aren't going to a court-martial. You are going to Christ, and when Christ asks you, 'What have you done for me?' what will you say?"

The military man's countenance changed. As he earnestly gazed at his friend, he answered with an anguish-filled, "*Nothing!* I have never done *anything* for Christ!"

His friend pointed out the awful mistake of habitually living with an awareness of our relationships with one another and forgetting our relationship to Christ and to God. The mistake is of thinking that doing no harm, or even doing good to those around you, will serve as a substitute for *living for God*. The big question is: *What have you done for Christ?*

> If this world is going to be reached, I am convinced it must be done by men and women of average talent.

Days later, he called on the old man again and asked, "Well, sir, what do you think now?"

The man replied, "I am a poor sinner."

He pointed him to the Savior of sinners, and not long afterward, he departed this life as a repentant sinner, resting in Christ. What an awful end would have come to the false peace in which he previously trusted. And yet it is this type of peace the multitudes trust in, but when they stand at the judgment seat of Christ they will find they were deceived.

If this world is going to be reached, I am convinced it must be done by men and women of average talent. After all, there are comparatively few people in the world who have great talents. One man has a single talent, another has three. I may have only half a talent. But if we all go to work and trade with the gifts we do have, the Lord will prosper us. We can double or triple our talents. We must be up and about our Master's work, every man building alongside his own house. The more we use the means and opportunities we have, the more our ability and our opportunities will be increased.

Consider this Eastern allegory. A merchant, going abroad for a time, gave two of his friends two sacks of wheat each, to take care of until he returned. Years passed, and when he came back he requested to see them. The first took him into a storehouse and showed them his sacks, but they were mildewed and worthless. The other led him out into the open country and pointed to field after field of waving grain, the produce of the two sacks given him. The merchant said, "You have been a faithful friend. Give me two sacks of that wheat. The rest will be yours."

I heard a person once say that she wanted assurance. I asked how long she had been a Christian. It had been a number of years. I said, "What are you doing for Christ?"

"I don't know that I have the opportunity of doing anything," she replied.

I pity the person who professes to be a Christian in these times, and who says he can't find opportunities for doing any work for Christ. The idea of anyone knowing the Lord Jesus Christ in this century, and saying he has no opportunities to testify for Him, is absurd. Surely, no one needs to look far to find plenty of opportunities for speaking and working for the Master, if he only has the desire to do it. *Lift up your eyes and look on the fields, for they are white already to harvest* (John 4:35). If you can't do some great thing, you can do some little thing.

A short time ago, a man sent me a tract titled *What is that in your hand?* and I am very thankful he sent it. These words were spoken by God to Moses when He called him to go down to Egypt and bring the children of Israel out of bondage. You remember how Moses tried to excuse himself. He said he wasn't eloquent – he wasn't this and that – and he couldn't go. Like Isaiah, he wanted the Lord to send someone else. Finally, the Lord said to Moses, "What is that in your hand?" He had a rod in his hand. It might have been that a few days before he had wanted something to drive the sheep with and he had cut this stick for that purpose. He could probably have gotten a hundred better rods any day. Yet with that rod, he was to deliver the children of Israel. God linked His almighty power with the rod and that was enough.

I can imagine that as Moses was on his way down to Egypt, he may have met one of the philosophers or freethinkers of his day, who might have asked him where he was going. "Down to Egypt."

"Really? Are you going down there again to live?"

"No, I'm going to bring my people out of bondage."

"What! You're going to deliver them from the hand of Pharaoh, the mightiest monarch now living? You think you are going to free three million slaves from the power of the Egyptians?"

"Yes."

"How are you going to do it?"

"With this rod."

What a contemptible thing the rod must have been in the eyes of that Egyptian freethinker. The idea of delivering three million slaves with a rod! We had three million slaves in this country, and before they could be set free, half a million men had to lay down their lives. The choicest of the nation marched to their graves before our slaves gained their deliverance.

Here was a weak and solitary man going down to Egypt to meet a monarch who had the power of life and death. All he had to deliver the people from bondage was this rod, but we see how famous that rod became. When Moses needed to bring up the plagues on Egypt, he just had to stretch out his rod and they covered the land. He only had to stretch it out and the water of the Nile turned into blood. Then when the people came to the Red Sea and they wanted to go across, he only had to lift up the rod and the waters separated, so the people could pass through on dry land. When they were in the desert and wanted water to drink, again he lifted this rod and struck the flinty rock, causing the water to burst forth, and they drank and were refreshed. That contemptible rod became mighty to be sure. But it wasn't the rod – it was the God of Moses, who humbled Himself to use it.

Let us learn a lesson from this history. We are required to use what we have – not what we don't have. Whatever gifts or talents you have, take and lay them at the Master's feet. Moses took what he had; and we see how much he accomplished. If we are ready to say, "Here am I, ready and willing to be used," then the Lord will use us. He will link His mighty power with our weakness, and we will be able to do great things for Him.

Look again and see Joshua as he goes up to the walls of Jericho. If you had asked what the Israelites had to bring down the walls of that city, it would have been only a few rams' horns. They must have looked poor and detestable in the eyes of the men of Jericho. Perhaps the city contained some men who were giants. As they looked over the walls and saw the Israelites marching around the city blowing these horns, they must have appeared very insignificant. But God can use the base things, the despised things. However contemptible a ram's horn may have appeared in the sight of man, the people went on blowing them as they were commanded. At the appointed time, down came the walls, and the city was taken. The Israelites had no battering rams, no great armor or mighty weapons of any kind. They simply took what they had, and God used it to do the work.

Look at Samson going out to meet a thousand Philistines. What does he have with him? Only *the jawbone of an ass* (Judges 15:16). If God could use that, surely He can use us, can't He? There isn't a person young or old whom He can't use, if we are willing to be used.

When I was in Great Britain ten years ago, I heard a Scotchman say that there probably wasn't a man in all Saul's army who didn't believe God *could* use him to go out and slay the giant of Gath. But there was only one solitary man who believed God *would* use him. David went out to meet Goliath, and we know the result.

We all believe that God *can* use us, but we need to take a step further and believe He *will* use us. If we are willing to be used, He is willing to use us in His service. How contemptible the smooth stones David took out of the brook would have appeared to Goliath. Even Saul wanted David to take his armor and put it on. He came close to doing that, but instead took his sling and the five smooth stones and went out. The giant of Gath fell before him. Let us go forth in the name of the God of hosts, using what we have, and He will give us the victory.

When I was in Glasgow a few years ago, a friend was telling me about an open-air preacher who since then has gone to be with the Lord. One Sunday morning this man preached on Shamgar. *And after him was Shamgar, the son of Anath, who slew of the Philistines six hundred men with an ox goad, and he also saved Israel* (Judges 3:31). He said, "I can imagine that when he was ploughing in the field a man came running over the hill all out of breath shouting, 'Shamgar! Shamgar! There are six hundred Philistines coming toward you!' Shamgar quietly said, 'You pass on, I can take care of them. They are four hundred short.' So he took an ox goad and slew some and routed the rest, and the Israelites fulfilled before their eyes the words, *one chase a thousand and two put ten thousands to flight* (Deuteronomy 32:30)." Nowadays, it takes about a thousand to chase one, because we don't realize we are weak in ourselves and that our strength is in God.

We need to remember that it's as true today as it ever was that one will chase a thousand. What we need is Holy Spirit power that uses the weakest child and makes him mighty in God's hand. **God puts aside the iron** Consider a mountain to be threshed, **and uses the worm to** a bar of iron lying there, and a little **thresh the mountain.** weak worm. God puts aside the iron and uses the worm to thresh the mountain. That's God's way. His thoughts are not our thoughts. His plans are not ours. *For my thoughts are not as your thoughts, neither are your ways as my ways* (Isaiah 55:8).

We say, "If such and such a man were only converted – that rich man or that wealthy lady – how much good could be done." Very true, but it may be that God will pass them by and use some poor tramp and make him the greatest instrument for good in all the land. John Bunyan, the poor Bedford tinker, was worth more than all the nobility of his day. God took him in hand, and he became mighty. He wrote that wonderful book, *The Pilgrim's Progress*, which has marched through the nations, lifting up many weary hearts, and cheering many who are discouraged and disheartened. If we are willing to be used, God is willing and waiting to use us.

I once heard an Englishman speak about Christ feeding the five thousand with the five barley loaves and the two small fish. He said that Christ may have taken one of the loaves and broken off a piece and given it to one of the disciples to divide. When the disciple began to pass it around he only gave a very small piece to the first, because he was afraid it wouldn't be enough. But after he gave the first piece, it didn't seem to grow any smaller. The next time he gave a larger piece, and still the bread wasn't depleted. The more he gave, the more the bread increased, until all had plenty.

Before they started feeding the multitudes, all the food could be carried in one basket. Once the whole multitude had been satisfied, the disciples gathered up twelve baskets full of leftovers. They had a good deal more when they finished than when they began. Let's be sure to bring our little barley loaves to the Master so He can multiply them.

You say you haven't got much? Well, you can use what you have. The longer I work in Christ's vineyard the more convinced I am that many people are kept out of the service of Christ – deprived of the luxury of working for God – because they are trying to do some great thing. Be willing to do little things. Remember that nothing is small when God is in it. Elijah's servant came to him and told him he saw a cloud not larger than a man's hand. That was enough for Elijah. *Then Elijah said to Ahab, Go up, eat and drink; for there is a sound of abundance of rain* (1 Kings 18:41). Elijah knew that the small cloud would bring rain. Nothing we do for God is small.

Some years ago, I met a young lady at the house where I was staying. She told me she had a Sunday afternoon class to teach in a mission school. At one of our afternoon meetings, I saw this lady sitting right up front. She must have arrived early to get a good seat. After the service, back at the house, I met up with her and said, "I saw you at the meeting today. I thought you had a class."

"So I do."

"Did you get someone to take it for you?"

"No."

"Did you tell the superintendent you weren't going to be there?"

"No."

"Do you know who had the class?"

"No."

"Do you know if anyone attended?"

"I am afraid there was nobody, because I saw a good many of the teachers of the school at your meeting."

"Is that the way you do the Lord's work?"

"Well, you know, I have only five little boys. I didn't think it would make any difference."

Only five little boys. Why, there might have been a John Knox, or a Wesley, or a Whitefield, or a Bunyan there. You can't know what these boys might become. One of them might become another Martin Luther. There might be a second Reformation asleep in one of these five little boys. It's an important thing to take "five little boys" and train them for God and for eternity. Such work can set a stream in motion that will flow on after you are dead and gone.

> **There might be a second Reformation asleep in one of these little boys.**

Little did the mother of the Wesleys know what would result when she trained her boys for God and for His kingdom. See what enormous results have flowed from that one source. It is estimated that there are twenty-five million members of the Methodist faith today, and over five million people who pass on the good news. It is estimated there are 110,000 regular and local preachers in the United States alone. Two new churches are being built every day of the year, and the work of the Methodist church is spreading over this great republic. And all this has been done in about a hundred and fifty years. Don't let mothers think their work of training children for God is a small one. In the sight of God, it is very important, and the result may be that many rise up in eternity to call them blessed.

Another mother who comes to mind has twelve boys. They've

all grown up to be active Christians. A number of them are preachers of the gospel, and all of them are true to the Son of God. Very few women in our country have done more for the nation than that mother. It is a great thing to be permitted to touch God's work and to be a co-worker with Him.

A bridge over the Niagara River is one of the great highways of the nation. Trains pass over it every few minutes of the day. When they began to build the bridge, the first thing they did was to take a boy's kite and send a little thread across the stream. It seemed a very small thing, but it was the beginning of a great work. In the same way, if we only lead one soul to Christ, eternity alone can tell what the result of that conversion will be. You may be the means of saving someone who will go on to be one of the most distinguished men in the service of God that the world has ever seen.

We may not be able to do any great thing, but if each of us will do *something*, however small it may be, very much will be accomplished for God. For many years, I've made it a rule not to let a single day pass without speaking to someone about eternal things. I started this habit years ago, and if I live the life allotted to man, there will be 18,250 people spoken to personally by me. That of course doesn't take into account those to whom I speak publicly. How often we as Christians meet with people and might be able to turn the conversation onto a path that will lead them to Christ.

Burdened hearts are all around us. Can't we help remove these burdens? I've heard someone represent this world as two great mountains – a mountain of sorrow and a mountain of joy. If each day we take something from the mountain of sorrow and add it to the mountain of joy, a lot will be accomplished in the course of a year.

A few days ago, I heard Mr. Spurgeon talking about when Moses went to tell the king of Egypt that he would call the plague of frogs upon the land. The king may have said, "Your God is the God of frogs, is He? I am not afraid of them. Bring them on. I don't care about the frogs!"

Moses says, "But there will be very many of them, O king." And he found that out.

We may be weak and contemptible individually, but there are a good many Christians scattered all over the land, and we can accomplish a great amount between us. Suppose each person who loves the Lord Jesus resolved today, with God's help, to try and lead one soul to Christ this week. Is there a professing Christian who can't lead some soul into the kingdom of God? If you can't, I need to tell you that there's something wrong in your life. You had better straighten it out right now. If you don't have an influence for good over someone among your friends or neighbors, then something in your life needs to be put right. May God show it to you today.

I can't understand the idea that a Christian man or woman has to live for years before they can have the privilege of leading anyone out of the darkness of this world into the kingdom of God. I also don't believe that all God's work is going to be done by ministers and other officers in the churches. This lost world will never be reached and brought back to loyalty to God until the children of God wake up to the fact that they have a mission in the world. If we are true Christians, we should all be missionaries. Christ came from heaven on a mission, and if we have His Spirit in us, we will be missionaries too. If we have no desire to see the world discipled – to see man brought back to God – there's something very wrong in our walk of faith.

If you can't work among older people, you can go to work among the children. We need Christians who can speak kindly to these boys and girls about their souls. It is something they will remember all their lives. They may forget the sermon or a Sunday school lesson, but if someone speaks to them personally, they will say, "That man or woman must be greatly interested in me, or they wouldn't have gone to the trouble to speak to me." They may wake up to the fact that they have immortal souls, and even if the preaching goes right over their heads, a little personal effort can be a blessing to them.

This personal and individual dealing with others is perfectly scriptural. Philip was called away from a great work in Samaria to go and speak to one man in the desert. Christ's conversation about being born again was addressed to one man, Nicodemus.

Don't let Satan make you believe children are too young to be saved. He said to him, *Verily, verily, I say unto thee, Except a person be born again from above, he cannot see the kingdom of God* (John 3:3). And that wonderful discourse by our Lord about the Water of Life was spoken to one poor sinful woman at the well. I pity those Christians who aren't willing to speak to one person. They're not fit for God's service. We won't accomplish much for God in the world if we aren't willing to speak to one or two people.

Another thing: Don't let Satan make you believe children are too young to be saved. Of course, you can't expect to put old heads on young shoulders. You can't make them into deacons and elders all at once. But they can give their young hearts to Christ.

Years ago, I ran a mission school in Chicago. The children were mostly from families with ungodly parents. I only had these children for about an hour out of the week, and it seemed as if any good they got was wiped out during the week. I used to think that if I ever became a public speaker, I would go all around the world and plead with parents to consider the importance of training their children for God and eternity.

On one of the first Sundays I traveled to Chicago, I stressed this to the congregation. When I finished my address, an old white-haired man got up. I was a bit nervous, thinking he was going to criticize what I had said. Instead, he said, "I want to give my support to all this young man has spoken. Sixteen years ago, I was in a pagan country. My wife died and left me with three motherless children. The first Sunday after her death my eldest girl, ten years old, said, 'Papa, may I take the children into the bedroom and pray with them like Mother used to do on Sunday?' I said she could.

"After some time, when they came out of the room, I saw that my eldest daughter had been weeping. I called her to me and said, 'Nellie, what's the problem?'

"She replied, 'Oh, Father, after we went into the room I said the prayer Mother taught me to say. Then [naming her little brother], he said the prayer that Mother taught him. Little Susie didn't used to pray when Mother took us in there because Mother thought she was too young. But when we got done, she said a prayer of her own. I couldn't help but weep when I heard her pray. She put her little hands together and closed her eyes and said, 'O God, you have taken away my dear Mama, and I have no mama now to pray for me. Won't you bless me and make me good just as Mama was, for Jesus Christ's sake? Amen.'"

"Little Susie gave evidence of having given her young heart to God before she was four years old. For sixteen years, she has been at work as a missionary among the unbelieving pagans."

Let us remember that God can use these little children. William Milnor was brought up a Quaker, became a distinguished lawyer in Philadelphia, and was a member of Congress for three successive terms. Returning to his home on a visit during his last congressional session, his little daughter rushed up to him exclaiming, "Papa! Papa! Did you know I can read?"

"No," he said, "let me hear you!"

She opened her little Bible and read: *Thou shalt love the Lord thy God with all thy heart* (Luke 10:27). It worked like an arrow in her father's heart, for it came to him as a serious admonition. *Out of the mouth of children* (Matthew 21:16), God's Spirit moved within him. He was driven to his closet, and a friend calling on him found he had been weeping over a Christian religious booklet titled *The Dairyman's Daughter*. Although only forty years of age, he abandoned politics and law for the ministry of the gospel, and for thirty years he served as the beloved pastor of St. George's Church in Philadelphia, the predecessor of the venerated Stephen Tyng.

Dear mothers and fathers, let us bring our children to Christ in simple faith. He is the same today as when He took children in His arms and said, *Suffer the little children to come unto me and forbid them not, for of such is the kingdom of the heavens* (Matthew 19:14).

> I may not do much with all my care,
>   But I surely may bless a few;
> The loving Jesus will give to me,
>   Some work of love to do;
> I may wipe the tears from weeping eyes,
>   I may bring the smile again
> To a face that is weary and worn with care,
>   To a heart that is full of pain.
>
> I may speak His name to the sorrowful,
>   As I journey by their side;
> To the sinful and despairing ones
>   I may preach of the Crucified.
> I may drop some little gentle word
>   In the midst of some scene of strife;
> I may comfort the sick and the dying
>   With a thought of eternal life.
>   – *Marianne Farningham*

Chapter 7

"She Has Done What She Could." (Mark 14:8)

I n Mark 14:1-9 we read: *Two days after was the passover and the days of unleavened bread; and the princes of the priests and the scribes sought how they might take him by craft, that they might kill him. But they said, Not on the feast day, lest there be an uproar of the people. And he being in Bethany in the house of Simon the leper, sitting at the table, there came a woman having an alabaster box of ointment of spikenard very precious; and breaking the alabaster, she poured it over his head. And there were some that had indignation within themselves and said, Why was this waste of the ointment made? For it might have been sold for more than three hundred denarius and given to the poor. And they murmured against her. But Jesus said, Let her alone; why trouble ye her? She has wrought a good work on me. For ye have the poor with you always, and whenever ye will, ye may do them good; but me ye have not always. She has done what she could, for she has anticipated anointing my body for the burial. Verily I say unto you, Wherever this gospel shall be preached throughout the whole world, this also that she has done shall be spoken of for a memorial of her.*

In John's gospel it says, *Jesus, therefore, six days before the passover, came to Bethany, where Lazarus was who had been dead, whom he raised from the dead. There they made him a supper; and Martha served, but Lazarus was one of those that sat at the table with him. Then Mary took a pound of ointment of spikenard, very costly, and anointed the feet of Jesus and wiped his feet with her hair; and the house was filled with the odour of the ointment. Then said one of his disciples, Judas Iscariot, Simon's son, who should betray him, Why was this ointment not sold for three hundred denarius and given to the poor? This he said, not that he cared for the poor, but because he was a thief and had the bag and would take from what was put therein. Therefore Jesus said, Let her alone; against the day of my burying she has kept this; for the poor ye always have with you, but ye shall not always have me* (John 12:1-8).

This is the last time we have a glimpse of the family of Mary and Martha at Bethany. It was Christ's last week there, and here we have the last recorded discussion between Christ and that lovely family.

Speaking of Martha and Mary, someone has said, "They were both dear to Jesus, and they both loved Him – but they were different. The eye of one saw His weariness and gave to Him. The faith of the other held on to His fullness and gained from Him. Martha's service was acceptable to the Lord and was acknowledged by Him, but He wouldn't allow it to disturb Mary's fellowship with Him. Mary knew His mind. She had deeper fellowship with Him. Her heart clung to Him."

I want to call your attention especially to one clause from the fourteenth chapter of Mark. *She has done what she could* (Mark 14:8). If someone had reported in Jerusalem that something was going to happen at Bethany on that memorable day that would outlive the Roman Empire and all the monarchs that ever existed or would exist, great excitement would have filled the city. People would have gone down to Bethany that day to see the thing about to happen – the miracle that was to live on for so long. Little did Mary think she was going to initiate a testimonial which would outlive empires and kingdoms. She never thought of herself. Love doesn't think of itself. What did **Love doesn't think of itself.** Christ say? *Wherever this gospel shall be preached throughout the whole world, this also that she has done shall be spoken of for a memorial of her* (Mark 14:9).

This one biblical account has already been put into 350 different languages, and it is now in circulation in every nation under heaven. Day by day this story is being printed and published. One society in London alone runs their presses every working hour of the day printing five hundred copies of this act of love that took place at Bethany. It is being spread to all the corners of the earth and will be told as long as the church of God exists. Matthew speaks of it and so do John and Mark.

Men seek to erect some memorial that will live on after they are dead and gone. This woman never thought about that. She simply wanted to lavish her love on Christ. But the act has lived on and will continue to live on while the church is on earth. It is even fresher today than it was a hundred years ago. In fact, there's never been a time when it's been as well known as today.

Although Mary was unknown outside of Bethany when she performed this act, now what she did is known all over the world. Kings have come and gone and empires have risen and crumbled. Egypt, with its ancient glories, has passed away. Greece, with its wise men, its mighty philosophers, and its warriors has been almost forgotten. The great Roman Empire has passed away. We don't know the names of those buried in the Pyramids, or those embalmed in Egypt with so much care and trouble, but the record of this humble life continues to be an inspiration to others.

Here is a woman whose memory has outlived Caesar, Alexander, Cyrus, and all the great warriors of the ancient world. We don't know if she was wealthy or beautiful or gifted or great in the eyes of the world. What we do know is that she loved the Savior. She took this box of precious ointment and broke it over the body of Christ. Someone has said it was the only thing He ever received that He didn't give away. It was a small thing in the sight of the world. If there had been daily newspapers in those days, and some Jerusalem reporter had been looking for interesting news to report to the people living there, he probably wouldn't have thought it newsworthy. Yet it has outlived all that happened in that century, except, of course, for the sayings and the other events connected with the life of Christ. Mary had Christ in her heart as well as in her faith. She loved Him and she showed her love in acts.

Thank God, every one of us can love Christ, and we can all do something for Him. It can be a small thing, but whatever it is, it will be lasting. It will outlive all the monuments on earth. The iron and the granite will rust and crumble and fade away, but anything done for Christ will never fade. It will be more lasting than time itself. Christ said, *The heaven and the earth shall pass away, but my words shall not pass away* (Luke 21:33).

Look again at that widow in the temple. Christ stood there as people passed by and threw their offerings into the treasury. The widow only had two mites and she threw it all in. The Lord saw her heart was in it, and so He commended her. If some nobleman had cast in a thousand dollars, Christ probably wouldn't have noticed it, unless his heart had gone with it. Gold is of little value in heaven. It is so plentiful there that they use it to pave the streets, and it is transparent gold, much better gold than we have in this world. It is when the heart goes with the offering that it is accepted by Christ. Accordingly, Jesus said, *I say unto you that this poor widow has cast in more than they all* (Luke 21:3). She had done all she could.

I think this is the lesson we are to learn from these Scripture accounts. The Lord expects us to do what we can. We can all do something. In one of our Southern cities, a few Christian people gathered together at the beginning of the war to see what could be done to build a church in a part of the city where the poor were very much neglected. After they discussed the matter, they wanted to see how much could be raised from the congregation.

One by one, the people agreed to give a certain amount, but they only got about half the amount needed. They thought they would have to abandon the project, but a washerwoman who sat way back in the meeting rose and said her little boy had died a week before. All he had was a gold dollar. She said, "It is all I have, but I will give the dollar to the cause." Her words touched the hearts of many. Rich men were ashamed at what they had given, and within a very short time, the whole amount was raised. I have spoken in that church, and today it is a center of influence in one of our great cities. This poor woman did what she could. Perhaps she gave more in proportion than anyone in the city.

When we were in London eight years ago, we wanted the city to be canvassed. We called for volunteers to go and visit people in their homes and invite them to come to the meetings. Among those who came forward was an old woman, eighty-five years of age. She said she wanted to do a little more for the Master before she went home. She took a district and went from house to house, delivering the invitation and tracts to the people. I suppose she has now gone to her reward, but I will never forget her. She wanted to do what she could. If every

Christian man and woman will do what Mary did, multitudes will be reached and blessed.

Years ago, when Illinois was just a young state, only a few settlers lived scattered here and there throughout a large portion of the state. One of these was a man who used to spend his Sundays hunting and fishing. He was an irreverent and notoriously wicked man. His little girl went to Sunday school in a log schoolhouse. There she was taught the way into the kingdom of God. When she was converted, the teacher tried to tell her how she might be used of God in doing good to others, and she thought she would begin with her father.

Others had tried to reach him and failed, but his own child had more influence with him. It is written, *a child shall shepherd them* (Isaiah 11:6). She got him to promise to go to the meeting. He came to the door, but wouldn't go in at first. He had gone to the school when he was young, but one day the boys laughed at him because he had a little speech impediment. After that, he'd decided never to go back, and as a result, he never learned to read.

However, he was now persuaded to go to the Sunday school. Once inside, he heard about Christ and was converted to God. His little child helped him, and others helped him. Soon he learned to read. This man has since died and been called to his reward, but about two years ago, when I saw him last, that man had established between eleven hundred and twelve hundred Sunday schools on the Western prairies. In addition to all these schoolhouses scattered across the country, churches have sprung up. Hundreds of flourishing churches have now grown out of these little mission schools he planted. He used to have a Sunday school horse, a "Robert Raikes" horse he called him, on which he traveled up and down the country going into outlying districts where nothing was being done for Christ. He used to gather parents into the log schoolhouses and tell how his little girl led him to Christ. I have heard a great many orators, but I never heard any who could move an audience like he could. He had no impediment in his speech when he began to speak for Christ. Instead, he had all the eloquence and fire of heaven. That little girl did what she could. She did a good day's work when she led her father to the Savior.

Every one of us can do something. If we are just willing to do what we can, the Lord will consent to use us, and it will be a great thing to be an instrument in His hand so He can do with us what He will.

I remember reading in the papers that when the theater in Vienna, Austria was on fire a few years ago, a man in one of the corridors was hurrying out. Many of the people tried to find their way out to escape from the fire, but it was dark. This man had a single match in his pocket. He struck it, and by doing so, he was able to save twenty lives. He did what he could.

> If you are the channel of saving one soul, you can be instrumental in saving a hundred more.

You think you can't do much? If you are the channel of saving one soul, you can be instrumental in saving a hundred more. When we were in England ten years ago, a woman in the city where we labored got stirred up for the Lord. It was this verse that moved her: *She has done what she could.* As a nominal Christian for many years, she didn't think she had any particular purpose in the world. I'm afraid that's the condition of many professed Christian men and women. Now she looked around her to see what she could do. She decided to try and do something for her fallen sisters in that town, and went out and began to talk kindly to those she met on the street. She rented a house and invited them to come and meet her there.

When we went back to that city about a year or so ago, she had rescued over three hundred of these fallen young women living on the streets and restored them to their parents and homes. She now corresponds with many of them. Think of more than three hundred of these sisters reclaimed from sin and death, through the efforts of one woman. She did what she could. What a grand harvest there will be, and how she will rejoice when she hears the Master say, *Well done, thou good and faithful slave* (Matthew 25:21).

I heard about a man in one of the hospitals who received a bouquet of flowers from the Flower Mission. He looked at the beautiful bouquet and said, "Well, if I'd known a bunch of flowers could do a person so much good, I would have sent flowers to the sick myself when I was well." If people only knew how they could cheer a lonely heart and lift up a sagging spirit, or speak some word that offers lasting effects forever, they would be out doing it. If the gospel is ever to be carried into the streets and alleys, up to the attics and down into the cellars, we must all be doing the work. As I have said, if each of us will do what we can, a great multitude will be gathered into the kingdom of God.

In illustrating the blessedness of cultivating a generous spirit, Reverend Dr. Willets, of Philadelphia, uses this beautiful illustration:

"See that little spring issuing water from the earth just in view on the distant mountain, shining like a thread of silver through the thick grove, and sparkling like a diamond in its healthy activity. It is hurrying on with tinkling feet to bear its tribute to the river. See, it passes a stagnant pool, and the pool hails it. 'Where are you going, master rivulet?'

"'I am going to the river to carry this cup of water God has given me.'

"'Ah, you are very foolish for that. You'll need it before the summer's over. Spring's weather has been going the wrong way and we will have a hot summer to make up for it. You will dry up then.'

"'Well,' said the rivulet, 'if I am to die so soon, I had better work while the day lasts. If I'm likely to lose this treasure from the heat, I'd better do good with it while I have it.' So, on it went, blessing and rejoicing in its course. The pool smiled complacently at its own superior foresight, and managed all its resources, not letting a drop steal away.

"Soon the midsummer heat came and fell upon the little stream, but the trees crowded to its brink and threw out their sheltering branches over it in the day of adversity, because it brought refreshment and life to them. The sun peeped through the branches and smiled complacently on its dimpled face as if to say, 'It's not in my heart to harm you,' and the birds sipped the silver tide and sung its praises.

"The flowers breathed their perfume on its heart and the farmer's eye sparkled with joy, as he looked at the streak of verdant beauty which marked its course through his fields and meadows, and so on it went blessing and blessed all.

"And where was the prudent stagnant pool? Sadly, in its glorious inactivity it grew sickly and produced infectious vapors. The beasts of the field put their lips to it, but turned away without drinking. The breeze stopped and kissed it by mistake, but shrunk away chilled. It caught malaria in the contact, and carried the sickness through the region. The inhabitants caught it and had to move away. In the end, even the frogs pitched their venom on the pool and deserted it. In mercy to man, heaven struck it with a hotter breath and dried it up.

"But the little stream didn't exhaust itself? Oh no. God saw to that. It emptied its full cup into the river and the river bore it on to the sea. The sea welcomed it, and the sun smiled on the sea. The sea sent up its spray to greet the sun, and the clouds caught it, and the winds, like waiting steeds, caught the chariots of the clouds and carried them away – away to the very mountain that gave the little fountain birth. There they tipped the brimming cup, and poured the grateful baptism down, and God saw to it that the little stream, though it gave so fully and so freely, never ran dry. And if God so blessed the stream, won't He bless you, if you have freely received, and so also freely give? Be assured He will."

A young lady belonging to a wealthy family was sent to a fashionable boarding school. In the school, Christ had a true witness in one of the teachers. She watched for an opportunity to reach some of the pupils. When this young lady of wealth and position came, the teacher set her heart on winning her to Christ. The first thing she did was to befriend her.

Let me say right here that we won't do much toward reaching people until we make them love us. This teacher, having won the heart of her pupil, began to talk to her about Christ, and she soon won her heart for the Savior.

> I pity those Christians who always ask if they have to give up this thing and that thing.

Then, instead of dropping her like so many do, she began to show her the privilege of working for God. They worked together and were successful in winning many of the young ladies in the school to Christ. When the pupil got a taste of work, that spoiled the world for her. To any Christian holding on to the world, you need to get into the Lord's work, and the world will soon leave you. Neither will you leave the work, because you'll have something much better than the world.

I pity those Christians who always ask if they have to give up this thing and that thing. You won't be asking that when you get a taste of the Lord's work. Then you'll have something the world can't give you.

When this young lady went back to her home, her parents were anxious for her to get out into worldly society. They gave many parties, but, to their great amazement, those didn't interest her. She hungered for something else. She went to the Sunday school in connection with the church she attended, and asked the superintendent to give her a class, but he said there were already more teachers than he needed.

She tried for weeks to find something to do for Christ. One day, as she walked down the street, she saw a little boy coming out of a shoemaker's shop. A man followed him out holding a wooden mold of a foot in his hand. He ran as fast as he could after the boy. When he realized he couldn't catch him, he hurled the mold at him and hit him in the back, but the boy kept running. When the shoemaker picked up his mold and returned to his shop, the boy stopped running and began to cry. The scene touched the heart of this young lady. When she reached the boy, she stopped and spoke to him kindly.

"Do you go to the Sunday school?"

"No."

"Do you go to the day school?"

"No."

"Why are you crying?"

He thought she was going to make fun of him, so he said it was none of her business. "But I am your friend," she said. He wasn't used to having a young lady like that speak to him. At first he was afraid of her, but in the end she won his confidence. Finally, she asked him to come to the Sunday school and be in her class.

"No," he said. "I don't like study." He wouldn't come.

"I won't ask you to study," she said. She told him she would tell him beautiful stories and they would sing. At last, he promised he would come. They agreed he would meet her on Sunday morning, at the corner of a certain street.

She wasn't sure he would keep his promise, but she was there at the appointed time – and he was there too. She took him to the school and said to the superintendent, "Can you give me a place where I can teach this boy?" He hadn't combed his hair and was barefooted. They didn't have any of that kind of children in the school. The superintendent looked at him, and said he didn't know just where to put him. Finally, he put him away in a corner, as far as he could from the others. There this young lady started her work that the angels would have been glad to do.

He went home and told his mother he thought he'd been among the angels. When she learned he'd gone to a Protestant school she told him he must not go again. When the father learned about it, he threatened to beat him every time he went to the school. However, the boy went again the next Sunday, and the father beat him. Every time he went, he gave the poor boy a beating. Finally, he said to his father, "I wish you would beat me before I go, and then I won't be thinking about it all the time I am at the school." You laugh at this, but let's remember that gentleness and love break down the opposition in the hardest heart. These little diamonds will sparkle in the Savior's crown, if we will just search them out and polish them. We can't make diamonds, but we can polish them.

Finding that the beatings didn't stop the boy from going to the school, the father said, "If you'll give up the Sunday school, I will give you every Saturday afternoon to play, or you can have all you make by peddling." The boy went to his teacher and said, "I have been thinking that if you could meet me on the Saturday afternoon we would have longer time together than on Sunday." I wonder if there is a wealthy young lady reading this book who would give up her Saturday afternoons to teach a poor little boy the way into the kingdom of God. She said she would gladly do it. If anyone came to see her on Saturdays, she was always engaged. It wasn't long before the light broke into the darkened mind of the boy and change came into his life. She bought him some good clothes and took an interest in him. She was a guardian angel to him.

One day he was down at the railway station peddling. He stood on the train platform and leaned against a railcar. When the engine gave a sudden start his foot slipped, and he fell under the train. It tragically passed over his legs. When the doctor came, the first thing the boy asked was, "Doctor, will I live to get home?"

"No, my boy, you are dying."

"Will you tell my father and mother that I died a Christian?"

Didn't the teacher get well paid for her work? She will be no stranger when she goes to heaven. That little boy will be waiting to welcome her.

It is a great thing to lead one soul from the darkness of sin into the glorious light of the gospel. I believe if an angel were to fly from earth up to heaven and say there was one poor, ragged boy, without father or mother, with no one to care for him and teach him the way of life – and if God asked who was willing to go down to this earth and live here for fifty years and lead that one to Jesus Christ – every angel in heaven would volunteer to go. Even Gabriel, who stands in the presence of the Almighty, would say, "Let me leave my high and lofty position, and let me have the luxury of leading one soul to Jesus Christ." There is no greater honor than being used as an instrument in God's hand for leading a person out of the kingdom of Satan into the glorious light of heaven.

> It is a great thing to lead one soul from the darkness of sin into the glorious light of the gospel.

I've written this motto in my Bible, and I recommend it to you:

> Do all the good you can,
> to all the people you can,
> in all the ways you can,
> and as long as ever you can.

If each of us immediately gets busy doing some work for God and will keep at it for 365 days in the year, then a good deal will be accomplished. Let's live in such a way that it can be truthfully said of us: We have done what we could.

Chapter 8

"Who Is My Neighbour?"
(Luke 10:29)

N o doubt you have frequently read the story of the good
Samaritan. In this parable, Christ highlights four men.
He draws the picture so vividly that the world will never for-
get it. Too often, when we read the Scripture narratives, they
don't reach our hearts, and before long we forget the lesson the
Master wants us to learn and remember.

We find that when Christ was on the earth a group of people
who gathered around Him continually found fault with everything He said and did. We read that on this occasion a lawyer
came asking Him what he could do to inherit eternal life. Our
Lord told him to keep the commandments – to love the Lord
with all his heart and his neighbor as himself. The lawyer asked,
who is my neighbor? Christ told him who his neighbor was and
what it was to love him.

It seems to me that we've been finding out who our neighbor
is for a long time. I think in the parable of the good Samaritan
Christ taught us very clearly that any man or woman who is
in need of our love and our help – whether worldly or spiritual

– is our neighbor. If we can provide them any service, we are to do it in the name of our Master.

At the start of this parable, we see two men. Each of them passed by a man in great need who had fallen among thieves and was stripped, wounded, and left to die. The first man to come down the road from Jerusalem to Jericho was a priest. As he went along the highway, he heard a cry of distress. He looked at the unfortunate man and could see that the poor suffering man was a Jew. Perhaps he'd seen him in the temple on the Sabbath. But then he wasn't in his own district now. His work was in the temple, and for now, it was finished. He was a professional man, and he had gone through all that was required of him. He was in a great hurry to get down to Jericho. It may be they were going to open a new synagogue there, and he was to dedicate it. A very important business, and, of course, he couldn't stop to help this poor wounded man lying on the side of the road. So he passed on.

Maybe as he went along, he reasoned with himself in this way: "I wonder why God ever permitted sin to enter the world at all. It is very strange that man would be in this fallen condition." Or his thoughts may have taken another turn. He may have said to himself that when he got down to Jericho he would form a committee to look after these unfortunate brothers. He would give something toward the expenses. Or he'd try and get a policeman to go and look after those thieves who stripped him. But all this time, he didn't think about the poor wounded man dying on the side of road who, by this time, was probably crying for water.

There might have been a brook running nearby to the spot where he lay that he couldn't get to. Yet this priest never stopped to give him a drink. His religion was all in his head and never reached his heart. The one thought in his mind was duty, duty. And when he finished with what he considered his duty, he believed his work was done. But God wants heart service. If we don't give Him that, we can give Him no service at all.

Next, we read that a Levite came along the highway where this wounded man lay in his helplessness. As he passed along, he also heard the man's cry of distress. He turned aside for a moment to look at the poor fellow, and he could see he was a son of Abraham – a brother Jew. But he also had to hurry on to Jericho. He possibly had to help in the ceremony of opening the new synagogue. Perhaps there was going to be a convention down there on "How to reach the masses," and he was going to help discuss the topic. I've noticed that many men nowadays will go to a conference and talk for hours on that subject, but they don't lift a hand to reach the masses themselves.

> I've noticed that many men nowadays will go to a conference and talk for hours on that subject, but they don't lift a hand to reach the masses themselves.

The Levite's thoughts probably took another turn. He might have said to himself, "I will see if I can't get a bill through the legislature to prevent those thieves from robbing and wounding people." Some people think they can legislate men back to God – that they can prevent sin through legislation. Like the priest, this Levite never stopped to give the poor man a drop of water to quench his thirst. He never attempted to bind his wounds or to help him in any way. He passed along the highway, probably saying something like, "I pity that poor fellow." Today we see a lot of that kind of pity, but it comes only from the lips, not from the heart.

The next one to come along that road was a Samaritan. Now in those days, a Jew wouldn't speak to a Samaritan. The very presence of the latter was considered a pollution to an orthodox Jew. No Jew ever entered the house of the hated Samaritan. He wouldn't eat at his table or drink from his well. Nor was a

Samaritan allowed to come under his roof. No religious Jew would even buy from or sell to a Samaritan. You know a Jew must have a very poor opinion of a person if he won't do business with him, when there is a prospect of making a profit from him.

Not only was this the case, but the Jews believed the Samaritans had no souls – that when they died they would be annihilated. Their graves were dug so deep that not even the sound of Gabriel's trumpet could wake them on resurrection morning. The Samaritan race was the only one under heaven that couldn't become proselytes to the Jewish faith and become members of the Jewish family. Repentance was denied them in this life and the life to come. Even if a Samaritan professed the Jewish religion, the Jews would have nothing to do with him. That was the way they looked at these Samaritans, yet Christ used the despised Samaritan to teach these bitter Jews the lesson of love to their neighbor.

In this parable, a third man came along. A Samaritan. It says that the priest *so happened* to come down that way – by chance, but we aren't told that the Samaritan came by chance. He represents our Lord and Master. We are told he came to where the poor wounded man lay, got off his beast, and stooped at the side of the wounded man. He looked at him and saw he was a Jew. If their roles had been switched, he would most likely have said, "Serves you right. I only wish the thieves had killed you outright. I wouldn't lift a finger to help you, you poor wretched Samaritan." But no. He didn't utter a word of criticism or blame.

Let's learn a lesson from this. Do you think drunkards need anyone to condemn them? There is no one in the wide world who can condemn them as they condemn themselves. What they need is sympathy – tenderness, gentleness, and kindness. This Samaritan didn't pull a manuscript from his pocket and begin to read a long sermon to the wounded man. Some people seem to think all the world needs is a lot of sermons. The truth is people today have been almost preached to death. What we want is to preach more sermons with our hands and feet – to carry the gospel to the people by acts of kindness.

Nor did he read this poor Jew a long lecture, endeavoring to prove that science is better than religion. He didn't give the injured man a long speech about what geology could do for him. What the poor man needed was sympathy and help. Therefore, the first thing the Good Samaritan did was to pour oil into his wounds. How many wounded men there are in our midst who have need of the oil of pity and sympathy, but many Christians seem to always carry a bottle of vinegar with them, which they bring out on all occasions.

> You have to come down to where they are and enter into their sorrows and troubles.

The Samaritan might have said to the man, "Why didn't you stay at Jerusalem? What business takes you down this road bringing about all this trouble?" Sometimes this is the type of thing said to a young man who has come to the city and gotten into trouble. They scold with words like, "Why did you ever leave your home and come to this wicked city?"

You are never going to reach people and do them good in that way, or by putting yourself above them. You have to come down to where they are and enter into their sorrows and troubles. See how this Samaritan *came where he was*, and instead of lecturing him, he poured the healing oil into his wounds.

Following are twelve things mentioned in Luke 10:30-37 that the Samaritan did. We can dismiss in a word all that the priest and the Levite did – they did *nothing*.

1. He *came where he was* (v. 33).

2. He *saw him* (v. 33), but he didn't pass by on the other side like the priest did.

3. He was *moved with compassion* (v. 33). If we want to be successful winners of souls, we too must be moved with compassion for the lost and the perishing. We must sympathize with men in their sorrows and troubles if we hope to gain their love and do them good.

4. He *went to him* (v. 34). The Levite went *near the place* where he was, but we are told that he, as well as the priest, *passed by on the other side* (vv. 31-32).

5. He *bound up his wounds* (v. 34). Perhaps he had to tear up his own garments in order to bind them up.

6. He treated the fainting man's wounds by *pouring in oil and wine* (v. 34).

7. He *set him on his own beast* (v. 34). Don't you think that this poor Jew must have looked on the Samaritan with gratitude and tenderness as he was placed on the beast and his deliverer walked by his side? All the prejudice in his heart must have disappeared long before they got to the end of their journey.

8. He *brought him to an inn* (v. 34).

9. He *took care of him* (v. 34). I was greatly touched at hearing about a Christian worker in one of the districts in London who met a drinking man at the meeting. He saw that the man had been drinking, so he took him home and stayed up all night with him. The next morning, when the man became sober, he talked with him. Many people are willing enough to talk with drunkards when they are sober, but how few go and hunt them up when they are

in their fallen condition, and stay with them until they can be reasoned with about their salvation.

10. *And on the morrow* he asked the host to *take care of him* (v. 35).

11. *He took out two denarius and gave them to the host* (v. 35).

12. He said, *whatever thou spendest more, when I come again, I will repay thee* (v. 35).

Nothing I can think of in all the teachings of Christ brings out the whole gospel better than this parable. It is a perfect picture of Christ coming to this world to seek and to save the lost.

1. He came to this world of sin and sorrow where we were, laying aside His glory for the time, so He might assume our human nature and put Himself on a level with those He came to save.

2. He mingled with the poor and needy so He could see their condition.

3. He was *moved with compassion* for the multitudes (Matthew 9:36). How often this is recorded in the Gospels. We are told, on more than one occasion, that He wept as He thought of all the anguish and distress sin had brought on the human family.

4. No cry of distress ever reached the ears of Jesus in vain. Wherever Jesus Christ heard about someone sorrowing or in need, He went at once.

5. On one occasion, He read from the prophets concerning Himself. *The Spirit of the Lord is upon me because he has anointed me . . . he has sent me to*

heal the brokenhearted (Luke 4:18). He Himself was wounded, so that the wounds which sin made in us might be bound up and healed.

6. He not only comforted the sorrowing, but He also gave the promise of the Holy Spirit, Who was to bring comfort and strength to His redeemed people.

7. In the same way the Good Samaritan set the wounded man on his own beast, the Savior gives us the unfailing promise of His Word on which we can rest during our pilgrim journey. He Himself has also promised to be with us in spirit along the way.

8. He brings us to the place of rest – rest in His love, in His willingness to save, in His power to keep us. In the end, He will bring us to the home of everlasting rest.

9. When He was on earth, He took a personal interest in all that concerned His disciples.

10. When He ascended into heaven, He sent another Comforter who would abide with believers making up Christ's church.

11. He has furnished the church with everything needed for her support and growth in grace. *All things that pertain to life and to godliness are given us of his divine power* (2 Peter 1:3).

12. He will come again and reward His servants for all their faithful service.

Do you want to know how you can reach the masses? Go to their homes and listen to them and feel what they are feeling. Tell them you have come to do them good, and let them see you have a heart that feels for them. When they find that you really care about them, all that's in their hearts against God and against Christianity will be swept out of the way. Atheists may tell them that you only want to get their money, and that you don't really care about their happiness. We have to contradict that lie by our lives – our example – and send it back to the pit where it came from.

We aren't going to do it unless we go personally to them and prove we really love them. Hundreds and thousands of families could easily be reached if we had thousands of Christians going to them in kindness and sympathy regarding their troubles. That is what they desire. This poor world is groaning and sighing for people to care. I am quite sure

> We aren't going to do it unless we go personally to them and prove we really love them.

it was that which touched the hearts of the common people in Christ's life. He made Himself one with them. He who was rich for our sakes became poor. He was born in the manger so He could put Himself on a level with the lowest of the low.

I think that, in this matter, He teaches His disciples a lesson. He wants us to convince the world that He is their friend, but they don't believe it. If the world grasped this thought, that Jesus Christ is the friend of the sinner, they would soon flock to Him. I am sure that ninety-nine in every hundred of those who are not *in Christ* think that, instead of loving them, God hates them. How are they to learn they are wrong? They don't attend our churches, and if they did, in many churches they wouldn't hear it.

Do you think if those poor prostitutes walking the streets of our cities really believed that Jesus Christ loved them and wanted to be their friend – that if He were here in person and didn't condemn them but took sides with them and tried to lift them up – that they would go on in their sins? Do you think the poor drunkard who reels along the street really believes Christ is his friend and loves him? The Scripture plainly teaches that even though Christ hates sin, He loves the sinner. This story of the good Samaritan is given to teach us this lesson. Let's proclaim the good news that Christ loves sinners and that He came into the world that He might save them.

A man who lived in one of our large cities died quite suddenly, and it wasn't long before his wife followed him to the grave. They left two boys as orphans and a wealthy citizen took the more promising of the boys and adopted him. The other boy was placed in the orphanage. He'd never been away from his father and mother while they were alive, and he'd never been separated from his brother. Every night, he fell asleep crying for his younger brother.

One night they couldn't find him. The next morning, they found him under the steps of the house of the wealthy banker who had adopted his little brother. When they asked him why he left a good comfortable bed at the orphan home to stay out there all night in the cold, he said, "I wanted to get near Charlie." He knew if he rang the bell and they found him at the door, they would send him back to the orphanage. It comforted him to be near Charlie, even if he had to pass the night out there. His young heart craved sympathy, and he knew Charlie loved him as no one else in the world did. If we can convince poor lost souls that someone loves them, their hearts will be moved.

During the war, a little boy, Frankie Bragg, was placed in one of the hospitals. He said, "It's so hard to be here away from everyone who loves me."

The nurse attending him bent down and kissed him and said, "I love you."

"Do you love me?" he asked. "That was like my sister's kiss. Kiss me again." The nurse kissed him again, and he smiled. "It's not hard for me to die now, when I know someone loves me." If we had more sympathy like this for the lost and the sorrowing, the world would soon feel our influence.

Can't we learn a lesson from the Good Samaritan? Let us hear the voice of the Master saying, *Go and do thou likewise* (Luke 10:37). We can all do something. If we can't reach the older people, let's try to win the young. It is a blessed privilege to be used of God to bring one little lamb into the kingdom. If we are the means of saving only one child, our life won't be a failure. We will hear the Master's voice: *Well done, good and faithful slave* (Matthew 25:23).

Two years ago, a lady started a hospital for sick, crippled children in Edinburgh. I asked her if she had been blessed in the work. I'll never forget how her face lit up. She attended one of our recent meetings in London, and her face beamed as she told some very interesting stories of conversion among the children. What a privilege to lead these suffering ones into the kingdom of God.

A little boy just six years old was brought to Edinburgh from Fife. There was no room in the children's hospital, and so they took him to the general hospital. His father was dead and his mother was so sick she couldn't care for him. They brought him to the hospital in Edinburgh where one day, my friend the Rev. George Wilson sat at the bedside of the little sufferer. He told him the doctor was coming on Thursday to take off his little leg.

You parents can imagine if your six-year-old child was away from home, in a hospital, and told that the doctor was coming on a certain day to take off his leg. He'd panic at the thought. Of course, the news greatly troubled this little fellow. The minister wanted to know about his mother, but learned she was sick and his father was dead. The minister longed to comfort the boy. He said, "The nurse is such a good woman. She will help you."

"Yes." The boy nodded. "And perhaps Jesus will be with me." Without a doubt, He was. The next Friday the man of God went to the hospital but found the boy's cot empty. The poor boy was gone. The Savior had come and taken him to heaven.

Aren't there hundreds and thousands in our great cities in some need of human sympathy? That sympathy will speak to their hearts much louder than eloquent sermons. Many won't be moved by an eloquent sermon, but will give in to tenderness, gentleness, and sympathy.

The great Dr. Thomas Chalmers said:

> The little that I have seen in the world and know of the history of mankind, teaches me to look on their errors in sorrow, not in anger. When I take the one poor heart that has sinned and suffered, and think to myself the struggles and temptations it has passed through – the brief pulsation of joy, the tears of regret, the feebleness of purpose, the scorn of the world that has little love, the desolation of the soul's sanctuary, threatening voices within, health gone, happiness gone – I would gladly leave the erring soul of my fellow man with Him from whose hands it came.

You may ask, "How am I to express sympathy to those in sorrow?" That is a very important question. Many people go to work for God, but they seem to do it in such a professional way. I will tell you how you can be brought to feel pity and sympathy. A rule which has proven to be of great help to me is to place yourself in the place of the sorrowing and afflicted ones with whom you want to sympathize. If you do, you'll soon gain their friendship and be able to help them.

God taught me a lesson a few years ago that I will never forget. I was superintendent of a Sunday school in Chicago with over fifteen hundred students. In the months of July and August, many deaths took place among the children, and as most of the ministers were out of the city, I had to attend a great many funerals. Sometimes I had to be at four or five in one day. I grew so used to it that I did it almost mechanically. I could watch the mother take her last look at the child, and see the coffin lid closed without being moved by it.

One day when I came home, my wife told me that one of the Sunday school children had been drowned, and the mother wanted to see me. I took my little daughter with me and we went to the house. I found the father in one corner of the room drunk. The mother told me that she took in washing in order to make a living for herself and her children, while her husband drank up all his wages. Little Adelaide used to go to the river and gather the floating wood for the fire. That day she had gone as usual. She saw a piece of wood out a little ways from the bank and as she stretched out to reach it, she slipped and fell into the water and drowned. The mother told me her sad story – how she had no money to buy the shroud and the coffin, and she wanted me to help her. I took out my notebook, wrote down her name and address, and the measurement of the coffin, in order to send it to the undertakers.

The poor mother was so distressed, but it didn't seem to move me. I told her I would be at the funeral, and then I left. As my little girl walked by my side, she said, "Papa, suppose we were very poor and Mama had to wash for a living, and I had to go to the river to get sticks to make a fire. If I were to fall into the water and get drowned, would you feel bad?"

"Feel bad! Why, I don't know what I would do. You are my only daughter, and if you were taken from me I think it would break my heart." I hugged her to my chest and kissed her.

"Then did you feel bad for that mother?"

How that question cut me to the heart. I went back to the house where the dead child's mother grieved and took out my Bible. I read the fourteenth chapter of John to her, and I prayed with her and did my best to comfort her. When the day for the funeral arrived, I attended it. I hadn't been to the cemetery for many years, because I had thought my time too precious, and it was miles away. There, I found the father was still drunk. As we were laying the coffin in the grave, another funeral procession came up, and the corpse was going to be laid nearby.

As we covered up the coffin with dirt, Adelaide's mother said, "Mr. Moody, it is very hard to lay her to rest here among strangers. I've moved about a good deal and have lived among strangers, and I have never had a burying lot. It's very hard to place my firstborn among strangers."

I said to myself that it would be pretty hard to have to bury my child in the strangers' field. By this time, I fully sympathized with the poor mother.

The next Sunday, I told the children in the Sunday school what had taken place. I suggested that we buy a Sunday school lot, and when any of the children attending the school died, they wouldn't have to be laid in the strangers' field, but would be put in our own lot. Before we could get the title made out, a mother came and wanted to know if her little girl who had just died could be buried in the lot. I gave permission, and I went to the funeral. As we lowered the little coffin, I asked her name. "Emma," the mother said. That was the name of my own little girl, and I couldn't help but weep as I thought of how I would feel if it were my own Emma.

Very soon afterward, another mother came and wished to have her dead child buried in our lot. His name was Willie, which at the time was the name of my only boy. I thought about how it would feel if it were my Willie who was dead. So, the first children buried there bore the names of my two children. I tried to put myself in the places of these sorrowing mothers, and then it became easy for me to sympathize with them in their grief, and to point them to Him who *shall wipe away all tears from their eyes* (Revelation 21:4).

About the first thing I did when I returned to Chicago nine years ago was to drive up to and see our children's lot. I thought it would take many years to fill that lot, but it was almost full, because many of my old Sunday school students had died while I'd been away and their bodies rested in this lot until the great day. However, I learned the children of the Sunday school were about to purchase another lot, larger than the first, which would suffice for many years under ordinary circumstances. Many little ones are laid there, waiting for the resurrection, and I would like to be buried beside them. How sweet it would be to be in their company when we rise and meet our Lord.

May God fill our hearts with the spirit of the Good Samaritan.

If you want to be fully sympathetic with others, put yourself in their place. May God fill our hearts with the spirit of the Good Samaritan, so we can be filled with tenderness, love, and compassion.

I want to share a motto with you that has been a great help to me. It was a Quaker's motto:

> "I expect to pass through this world but once. If, therefore, there be any kindness I can show or any good thing I can do to any fellow human being let me do it now. Let me not defer nor neglect it, for I will not pass this way again."

Chapter 9

"Ye Are the Light of the World." (Matthew 5:14)

And those that understand shall shine as the brightness of the firmament; and those that teach righteousness to the multitude as the stars in perpetual eternity. (Daniel 12:3)

This is the testimony of Daniel as an old man. He'd had the richest, deepest experience of any man living on the face of the earth at the time. As a young man, he was taken down to Babylon; some Bible scholars think he was no older than twenty years of age. As he was carried into captivity, if anyone had said he would outrank all the mighty men of that day – that all the generals victorious in almost every nation at that time were going to be surpassed by this young slave – probably no one would have believed it. Yet for five hundred years, no man whose life is recorded in history shined like this man. He outshined Nebuchadnezzar, Belshazzar, Cyrus, Darius, and all the princes and mighty monarchs of his day.

We aren't told when he was converted to a knowledge of the true God, but I think we have good reason to believe he had been brought under the influence of Jeremiah the prophet. Evidently, some sincere, godly man – not a worldly professor – made a deep impression upon him. At any rate, someone taught him how he was to serve God.

Nowadays, people talk about the difficulty of the field in which they work. They say their position is a very unique one. Think about the field in which Daniel had to work. He wasn't only a slave, but he was also held captive by a nation that detested the Hebrews. He didn't know the language and was among idolaters. Yet he began to shine right from the start. He took his stand for God from the very beginning, and that's how he went on to live his whole life. He gave the dew of his youth to God and continued faithfully on, until his pilgrimage on this earth ended.

> Notice all who have made a deep impression on the world and shone most brightly have been people who lived in a dark time.

Notice all who have made a deep impression on the world and shone most brightly have been people who lived in a dark time. Look at Joseph. He was sold as a slave into Egypt by the Ishmaelites. Yet he took his God with him into captivity, just like Daniel did after him. And he remained true to the end. He never gave up his faith, even though he had been taken away from home and placed among idolaters. He stood firm, and God stood by him.

Look at Moses. He turned his back on the gilded palaces of Egypt, and identified himself with his despised and downtrodden nation. If a man ever had a hard field, it was Moses, but still he shone brightly and never proved unfaithful to his God.

Elijah lived in a far darker day than we do. The whole nation was going over to idolatry. Ahab and his queen, and all the royal court were throwing their influence against the worship of the true God. Yet Elijah stood firm and shone brightly in that dark and evil day. How his name stands out on the pages of history.

Look at John the Baptist. I used to think I would like to live in the days of the prophets, but I have given up that idea. You can be sure that when a prophet appears on the scene, everything is dark and the professing church of God has gone over to the service of the god of this world. This is how it was when John the Baptist made his appearance, and see how his name shines out today. Eighteen centuries have rolled by, and the fame of that wilderness preacher shines brighter than ever. He was looked down upon in his day and generation, but he has outlived all his enemies. His name will be regarded with respect and fondness and his work remembered as long as the church is on the earth.

Talk about your field being a hard one, consider how Paul shone for God as he went out as the first missionary to the heathen, and telling them about the God he served and how He sent His Son to die a cruel death in order to save the world. Men hated him and his teachings. They laughed him to scorn when he spoke about the Crucified One. But he went on preaching the gospel of the Son of God. The great and mighty of his day regarded him as a poor tent maker, but today who can name any of his persecutors, or others who lived at that time, unless their names happen to be associated with his.

Now, the fact is, all men like to shine. We may as well acknowledge it right now. In business circles just watch how men struggle to get to the top. Everyone wants to outshine his neighbor and to stand at the head of his profession. Go into the political world and see the struggle going on to see who will be the greatest. If you go into a school, you find a rivalry among the boys and girls. They all want to stand at the top of the class. When a boy reaches this position, and outranks all the rest, his mother is very proud of him. She manages to tell all the neighbors how well Johnnie has done and all about the number of prizes he has been awarded.

You go into the army and you find the same thing – one trying to advance above the other. Everyone is very anxious to shine and rise above his comrades. Go among the young men in their games and see how anxious the one is to outdo the other. All these examples serve as reminders to us that we all have that desire in us. We like to shine above our companions and coworkers.

And yet very few can really shine in the world. Once in a while, one man will advance beyond all his competitors. What a struggle goes on throughout our country every four years to see who will be the president of the United States. The battle rages for six months or even a year. Yet only one man can get the prize. A good many struggle in this race to get the title, but many are disappointed because only one can attain the coveted prize. But in the kingdom of God, the very least and the very weakest can shine if they want. Not only can *one* obtain the prize, but *all* can have it if they want it.

In Daniel 12:3, it doesn't say that the statesmen are going to shine as the brightness of the firmament. The statesmen of Babylon are gone and their very names are forgotten. It says that *those that understand shall shine as the brightness of the firmament.*

It doesn't say that the nobility will shine. Earth's nobility are soon forgotten. John Bunyan, the Bedford tinker, has outlived all the nobility of his day. They lived for self, and their memory is blotted out. He lived for God and for souls, and his name is as fragrant as ever.

We aren't told that the merchants are going to shine. Who can name any of the millionaires of Daniel's day? They were all buried in oblivion a few years after their death. Who were the mighty conquerors of that day? Few can tell. It is true that we hear of Nebuchadnezzar, but we probably wouldn't have known much about him if it weren't for his interactions with the prophet Daniel.

When we look at this faithful prophet of the Lord, we see it is different. Twenty-five centuries have passed away, and his name shines on, and on, and on, brighter and brighter. And it is going to continue to shine while the church exists. *Those that understand shall shine as the brightness of the firmament; and those that teach righteousness to the multitude as the stars in perpetual eternity.*

How quickly the glory of this world fades away. Seventy-five years ago the great Napoleon almost made the earth tremble. How brightly he blazed and shone like an earthly warrior for a short while. A few years passed and the little island of Elba held that once proud and mighty conqueror in exile. He died as a poor brokenhearted prisoner. Where is he today? Almost forgotten. Who in all the world will say that Napoleon lives on fondly in their heart?

But look at Daniel. He was a despised and hated Hebrew prophet. They wanted to put him into the lions' den because they thought he was too self-righteous and too religious. Yet see how his memory lives on today. How his name is loved and honored for his faithfulness to his God.

Seventeen years ago, I was in Paris at the time of the Great Exhibition. Napoleon III was then in his glory. Cheer after cheer rose up as he drove along the streets of the city. A few short years later, he fell from his lofty position. He died an exile from his country and his throne, and where is his name today? Very few think about him at all, and if his name is mentioned, it is not with love and esteem. How empty and short-lived is the glory and pride of this world. If we are wise, we will live for God and for eternity. We will get outside of ourselves and care nothing about the honor and glory of this world.

In Proverbs we read: *he that wins souls is wise* (Proverbs 11:30). If any man, woman, or child wins one soul to God by a godly life and example, their life will not have been a failure. They will have outshone all the mighty men of their day, because they will have set a stream in motion that will flow on and on, forever and ever. That little boy may shine in God's kingdom if he wants.

God has left us down here to shine. We aren't here to buy, sell, and accumulate worldly possessions and wealth, or acquire position. This earth, if we are Christians, is not our home. It is up in heaven with the Lord. God has sent us into the world to shine for Him – to light up this dark world. Christ came to be the Light of the World, but people put out that light. They took it to Calvary and blew it out. Before Christ went up to heaven, He said to His disciples, *Ye are the light of the world* (Matthew 5:14). *Ye are my witnesses* (Isaiah 43:10). Go and carry the gospel to the perishing nations of the earth.

God has called us to shine, just like Daniel was sent into Babylon to shine. Let no man or woman say that they can't shine because they don't have as much influence as someone else may have. What God wants you to do is to use the influence you have. Daniel probably didn't have much influence when he first arrived in Babylon, but God soon gave him more, because he was faithful and used what he had.

Remember, a small light will do a good deal when it is in a very dark place. Put one little tallow candle in the middle of a large hall, and it gives very much light.

Away out in the prairie regions, when meetings are held at night in the log schoolhouses, the announcement of the meeting is given in this way: "A meeting will be held by early candlelight." The first man who comes brings a tallow-dip with him. It may be all he has, but he brings it and sets it on the desk. It doesn't light the building much, but it is better than nothing at all. The next man brings his candle, and the next family brings their candles. By the time the house is full, plenty of light brightens the room. In the same way, if we all shine a little, there will be a good amount of light. That is what God wants us to do. If we can't all be lighthouses, any one of us can at least be a tallow candle.

A little light will sometimes do very much. The city of Chicago was set on fire by a cow kicking over a lamp, and a hundred thousand people lost their homes and all their possessions. Don't let Satan get the advantage over you and make you think that because you can't do anything great, you can't do anything at all.

We are to *let* our light shine. It doesn't say, "*Make* your light shine." You don't have to *make* light shine. All you have to do is *let* it shine.

I heard about a man at sea who was very seasick. If there is a time when a man feels he can't do any work for the Lord – in my opinion – it is then. While sick like this, this man heard that another man had fallen overboard. He wondered if he could do anything to help save the man. He took hold of a light and held it up to the porthole. The drowning man was saved. When this man recovered from his seasickness, he went up on deck one day and there talked with the man who was rescued. The saved man gave this testimony. "I had gone down the second time, and was just going down again for the last time, when I put out my hand. Just then, someone held a light at the porthole, and the light fell on my hand. A man caught me by the hand and pulled me into the lifeboat."

> We are to *let* our light shine. It doesn't say, "Make your light shine."

It seemed a small thing to do – to hold up the light – yet it saved the man's life. If you can't do some great thing, you can hold the light for some poor, perishing drunkard who can be won to Christ and delivered from destruction. Let's take the torch of salvation and go into these dark homes, and hold up Christ to the people as the Savior of the world. If these perishing masses are to be reached, we must lay our lives right alongside theirs, pray with them, and work for them.

I wouldn't give much for a man's Christianity if he is saved but isn't willing to try and save others. It seems the vilest ingratitude if we don't reach out our hand to others who are down in the same pit from which we were delivered. Who is able to reach and help these drinking men like those who have been slaves to the intoxicating cup themselves? Won't you go out this very day and seek to rescue these people? If we were all to do what we can, we could soon empty the bars and taverns.

I read about a blind man who was found sitting at the corner of a street in a big city with a lantern beside him. Seeing that he was blind, someone asked why he had the lantern there, since for him, the light was the same as the darkness. The blind man replied, "I have it so no one can stumble over me."

Let's think about that. Where one man reads the Bible, a hundred read you and me. That is what Paul meant when he said, *Ye are our epistle written in our hearts, known and read of all men* (2 Corinthians 3:2). I wouldn't give much for what can be accomplished through sermons, if we don't preach Christ by our lives. If we don't declare the gospel to people by our sanctified walk and conversation, we won't win them to Christ. Some little act of kindness could perhaps do more to influence them than any number of long sermons.

A vessel caught in a storm on Lake Erie tried to make for the harbor of Cleveland. At the entrance of that port, they had what are called the upper lights and the lower lights. Away back on the bluffs the upper lights burned brightly enough, but when they drew near the harbor they couldn't see the lights showing the entrance. The pilot said he thought they had better get back on the lake again. The captain said he was sure they would go down if they went back, and he urged the pilot to do what he could to gain the harbor. The pilot said, "There's very little hope of making for the harbor, because I have nothing to guide me as to how I should steer the ship."

They tried all they could to get the ship into the harbor. She rode on the top of the waves and into the trough of the sea. Finally, they found themselves stranded on the beach, where the vessel was dashed to pieces. Someone had neglected the lower lights, and they had gone out.

Let us take this warning to heart. God keeps the upper lights burning as brightly as ever, but He has left us down here to keep the lower lights burning. We are to represent Him here, as Christ represents us up in heaven. I sometimes think if we had as poor a representative in the courts above as God has down here on earth, we would have a pretty poor chance of ever reaching heaven. Let us have our loins girded and our lights brightly burning, so others can see the way and not walk in darkness. *Having the loins of your understanding girded with temperance, wait perfectly in the grace that is presented unto you when Jesus, the Christ, is manifested unto you, as obedient sons, not conforming yourselves with the former desires that you had before in your ignorance, but as he who has called you is holy, so be ye holy in all manner of conversation* (1 Peter 1:13-15).

Speaking of a lighthouse reminds me of what I heard about a man in the state of Minnesota who, some years ago, was caught in a fearful storm. That state is cursed with storms, which sweep down so suddenly in the winter that it makes escape difficult. The snow falls and the wind beats it into the face of the traveler so he can't see two feet ahead. Many a man has been lost on those prairies when caught in one of those storms.

This man was caught and almost at the point of giving up, when he saw a little light in a log house. He managed to get there and found a shelter from the fury of the tempest. He is now a wealthy man. As soon as he was able, he bought the farm and built a beautiful house on the spot where the log building stood. On the top of a tower he put a revolving light, and every night when a storm blows in, he lights it up in the hope that it can be used to save someone else.

That is true gratitude, and that is what God wants us to do. If He has rescued us and brought us up from the horrible pit, let us always look to see if there isn't someone else whom we can help save.

I heard about two men who had charge of a revolving light in a lighthouse on a storm-bound and rocky coast. Somehow the machinery broke, and the light didn't revolve. They were so afraid those at sea would mistake it for some other light that they worked all night manually rotating the light.

Let us keep our lights in the proper place, so that the world can see that the life in Christ isn't a sham but a reality. *Let your light so shine before men that they may see your good works and glorify your Father who is in the heavens* (Matthew 5:16). It is said that in the Grecian sports they had one game where the men ran with lights. They lit a torch at the altar and ran a certain distance. Sometimes they were on horseback. If a man came in with his light still burning, he won a prize, but if his light had gone out, he lost the prize.

How many there are who, in their old age, have lost their light and their joy. They once were brightly burning lights in the family, in the Sunday school, and in the church. But something has come between them and God – the world or self – and their light has gone out. If you have experienced this, I pray God helps you to come back to the altar of the Savior's love and lights your torch anew, so you can go out into the streets and alleys and let the light of the gospel shine in these dark homes.

As I have already said, if we only lead one soul to Jesus

Christ, we can set a stream in motion that will flow on when we are dead and gone. Away up the mountainside, there is a little spring. It seems so small that a single ox might drink it up in one draught. Before long, it becomes a rivulet, and other rivulets run into it. Gradually, it becomes a large brook, and then it becomes a broad river sweeping onward to the sea. On its banks are cities, towns, and villages, where many thousands live. Vegetation flourishes on every side and commerce is carried down its majestic center to distant lands.

So, if you turn one person to Christ, that one may turn a hundred, and they may turn a thousand, and so the stream, small at first, goes on broadening and deepening as it rolls toward eternity.

In the book of Revelation we read: *Blessed are the dead who die in the Lord from now on; Yea, saith the Spirit, that they may rest from their labours, and their works do follow them* (Revelation 14:13).

We read the names of many people in the Scriptures who lived such-and-such number of years and then they died. The cradle and the grave are brought close together in these accounts. They lived and they died, and that is all we know about them. In the same way, today you could write on the tombstone of a lot of professing Christians that they were born on such a day and they died on such a day – with nothing whatsoever in between.

Paul was never more powerful than he is today.

But there's one thing you can't bury with a good man: His influence still lives. They haven't buried Daniel's influence. It lives on today as great as ever. Do you tell me Joseph is dead? His influence still lives and will continue to live on and on. You can bury the frail tent of clay that a good man lives in, but you can't get rid of his influence and example. Paul was never more powerful than he is today.

Do you tell me that John Howard, who went into so many of the dark prisons in Europe, is dead? Is Henry Martyn, or William Wilberforce, or John Bunyan dead? Go into the Southern states and you'll find three to four million men and women who were once slaves. You mention to any of them the name of Wilberforce, and see how quickly their eyes light up. He lived for something besides himself, and his memory will never die out of the hearts of those for whom he lived and worked.

Are Wesley or Whitefield dead? The names of these great evangelists were never more honored than they are now. Is John Knox dead? You can go to any part of Scotland today, and you'll feel the power of his influence.

I can't tell you about those who are dead – the enemies of these servants of God – those who persecuted them and told lies about them. However, the great men I've mentioned have outlived all the lies spoken about them. Not only that, they will also shine in another world. The words of the old Book are so true. *Those that understand shall shine as the brightness of the firmament; and those that teach righteousness to the multitude as the stars in perpetual eternity* (Daniel 12:3).

Let's go on turning as many as we can to righteousness. Let us be dead to the world, to its lies, its pleasures, and its ambitions. Let's live for God, continually going forth to win souls for Him. Let me quote a few words by Dr. Chalmers.

> Thousands of men breathe, move, and live, pass off
> the stage of life, and are heard of no more. Why?
> they do not partake of good in the world, and none
> were blessed by them; none could point to them
> as the means of their redemption; not a line they
> wrote, not a word they spake could be recalled; and
> so they perished: their light went out in darkness,
> and they were not remembered more than insects

of yesterday. Will you thus live and die, O man immortal? Live for something. Do good, and leave behind you a monument of virtue that the storm of time can never destroy. Write your name, in kindness, love, and mercy, on the hearts of thousands you come in contact with year by year: you will never be forgotten. No! your name, your deeds, will be as legible on the hearts you leave behind as the stars on the brow of evening. Good deeds will shine as the stars of heaven.

About the Author

Dwight L. Moody, determined to make a fortune, arrived in Chicago and started selling shoes. But Christ found him and his energies were redirected into full-time ministry. And what a ministry it was. Today, Moody's name still graces a church, a mission, a college, and more. Moody loved God and men, and the power of a love like that impacts generations.

Similar Updated Classics

Are you an overcomer? Or, are you plagued by little sins that easily beset you? Even worse, are you failing in your Christian walk, but refuse to admit and address it? No Christian can afford to dismiss the call to be an overcomer. The earthly cost is minor; the eternal reward is beyond measure.

Dwight L. Moody is a master at unearthing what ails us. He uses stories and humor to bring to light the essential principles of successful Christian living. Each aspect of overcoming is looked at from a practical and understandable angle. The solution Moody presents for our problems is not religion, rules, or other outward corrections. Instead, he takes us to the heart of the matter and prescribes biblical, God-given remedies for every Christian's life. Get ready to embrace genuine victory for today, and joy for eternity.

Available where books are sold.

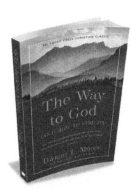

There is life in Christ. Rich, joyous, wonderful life. It is true that the Lord disciplines those whom He loves and that we are often tempted by the world and our enemy, the devil. But if we know how to go beyond that temptation to cling to the cross of Jesus Christ and keep our eyes on our Lord, our reward both here on earth and in heaven will be 100 times better than what this world has to offer.

This book is thorough. It brings to life the love of God, examines the state of the unsaved individual's soul, and analyzes what took place on the cross for our sins. The Way to God takes an honest look at our need to repent and follow Jesus, and gives hope for unending, joyous eternity in heaven.

Available where books are sold.

Printed in Great Britain
by Amazon

42438021R00082